D1600002

The Political Constitution

The Political Constitution

THE CASE AGAINST JUDICIAL SUPREMACY

Greg Weiner

University Press of Kansas

Published by the University Press of Kansas (Lawrence, Kansas 66045),
which was organized by the Kansas Board of Regents and is operated and
funded by Emporia State University, Fort Hays State University, Kansas
State University, Pittsburg State University, the University of Kansas, and
Wichita State University.

Library of Congress Cataloging-in-Publication Data

Names: Weiner, Greg, author.
Title: The political constitution : the case against judicial supremacy /
Greg Weiner.
Description: Lawrence : University Press of Kansas, 2019. | Includes
bibliographical references and index.
Identifiers: LCCN 2019007256
   ISBN 9780700628377 (cloth : alk. paper)
   ISBN 9780700628384 (ebook)
Subjects: LCSH: Political questions and judicial power—United States.
Classification: LCC KF5130 .W45 2019 | DDC 342.73/0412—dc23
LC record available at https://lccn.loc.gov/2019007256.

British Library Cataloguing-in-Publication Data is available.

Printed in the United States of America

10 9 8 7 6 5 4 3 2 1

The paper used in this publication is recycled and contains 30 percent
postconsumer waste. It is acid free and meets the minimum requirements
of the American National Standard for Permanence of Paper for Printed
Library Materials Z39.48-1992.

For Hannah, Jacob, and Theodore

In short, [the justices of the Supreme Court] are independent of the people, of the legislature, and of every power under heaven. Men placed in this situation will generally soon feel themselves independent of heaven itself.

Brutus

Contents

Acknowledgments

The debts accrued in writing this, as any, book are immense. Most of all, I am grateful to my wife, Rebecca, and my children, Hannah, Jacob, and Theodore, for their inspiration and patience. My colleagues Daniel J. Mahoney and Daniel P. Maher were generous, as they always are, with their editing and guidance. Marc Guerra's guidance on Aquinas was invaluable. Richard M. Reinsch II of Liberty Fund's Online Library of Law and Liberty provided the forum in which I have developed and tested many of these ideas. Adam J. White read and commented on the manuscript. Much of the material in chapter 3 was presented to Harvey C. Mansfield's Program on Constitutional Government at Harvard University. I am grateful to him as well as the participants for their challenges and suggestions. Judge J. Harvie Wilkinson III provided comments on an initial prospectus, as did Larry D. Kramer and John Agresto. Nicole Roy was a studious and patient research assistant. I am grateful to the University Press of Kansas's peer reviewers on both the prospectus and the manuscript, and to my editor, David Congdon, for his patient guidance. Finally, two late teachers, George W. Carey and Wallace Mendelson, indelibly shaped my constitutional views.

All errors are mine.

Introduction

This is not a book about constitutional meaning. It is a book about constitutional authority. People may disagree about the meaning of the Constitution without assuming its content is to be decreed by judges alone. It is also a book about politics in the largely lost and noble sense of that word. The thesis is that a political community is healthiest when it engages in decisions about common things as a coherent whole. The Romans called this the res publica—the public thing—and it is the root of the word "republic," so it is ironic at best that proponents of judicial engagement—the position that judges should be assertive in policing constitutional rights—have attempted to hijack "republican" to refer to a radical individualism in which the community has no claims on the individual and, indeed, has no ontological status at all.

I do not aspire in these pages to delineate a comprehensive theory of constitutionalism. The aim is more modest: it is a critique of judicial engagement. There have been many such critiques, of course, and many elucidations of various varieties of judicial restraint. Explicators of the latter include James Bradley Thayer, Robert H. Bork, Raoul Berger, Larry D. Kramer, Lino Graglia, Christopher Wolfe, Matthew J. Franck, George Thomas, Benjamin A. Kleinerman, Eugene W. Hickok and Gary L. McDowell, Robert P. George, John Agresto, J. Harvie Wilkinson III, James Stoner, and Mark Pulliam, among others.[1] Meanwhile, critics of restraint, or forms of it, have included Randy E. Barnett, Timothy Sandefur, Richard Epstein, Steven G. Calabresi, Richard Posner and Tara Smith, many of whom we shall encounter in the pages that follow.[2]

Of these, Thomas has most clearly elucidated the concept of a "political constitution" in the sense in which it is meant here. Deploying James Madison's thought, Thomas casts "the political framework" of the Constitution rather than the legal one "as primary." This suggests "that questions of constitutional interpretation be resolved as part of constitutional politics and often in the ordinary political process." On this view, shared here, the Supreme Court does not wield exclusive authority over constitutional meaning. Whereas the legal conception of the Constitution empowers the judiciary to enforce the text, "[t]he key to constitutional maintenance for Madison is the very structure the written constitution calls forth."[3] Keith Whittington, too, describes a "political constitution." Contemporary views of the Constitution equate judicial review with constitutionalism. "This image, though dominant, obscures too much. The Constitution penetrates politics, shaping it from the inside and altering the outcomes. Along the way, the Constitution is also made subject to politics." Whittington describes the Constitution as political insofar as its political mechanisms participate in "constitutional construction," which he defines as "the method of elaborating constitutional meaning in this political realm."[4]

The "political constitution" presented in the pages that follow is largely compatible with, and indebted to, these other conceptions. But it seeks to move beyond the important notion that political mechanisms are involved in settling constitutional meaning to recuperate a classical conception of politics that infuses and is enabled by the architecture of the Constitution. The judiciary plays a part, but only that, in this process. The Constitution, in addition to setting the rules of the political game, preserves space for a politics of interdependence and obligation that chapter 2 seeks to elucidate more fully.

Corinna Barrett Lain is one of a handful of legal theorists who have proposed that the Supreme Court on occasion actually acts as the more majoritarian branch of government, constitutionalizing national consensuses that the political process fails to enact. However, Lain's model of "upside-down judicial review" refers to majority consensus on policy issues, not constitutional ones (for example, she notes that a national majority was pro-choice at the time of *Roe v. Wade* but does not present evidence on the issue with which republican constitutionalism is concerned: whether that majority had contemplated the constitutional issues involved in the case). Moreover, she assumes that the constitutional purpose of legislatures is to enact the views of majorities as reflected in opinion polling, and that the counter-majoritarian difficulty is overcome if the courts do so instead. But what I shall call "republican constitutionalism" would also assume that the constitutional purpose of legislatures is to instantiate the *deliberate* views of the people, so polling at any moment in time would not license the Supreme Court to override legislatures.[5]

What I hope to add to this debate is a political case for the restraint of judicial authority. That is different, as we shall see, from judicial *self-restraint*: judges should behave no more assertively than the Constitution authorizes, but to rely on self-restraint alone is to separate them from the rest of the Constitution's architecture. The case is political insofar as it follows Aristotle in assuming political life to be good and necessary for human beings. It is not, I hope, a romantic case. To say Athens and Rome are unrecoverable is not to say America should continue a slide away from republicanism and toward judicial superintendence.

In calling this a book about constitutional authority, I of course do not mean to dismiss the importance of constitutional meaning. On the contrary, they are inextricable insofar as the extent of judicial authority is itself a question of constitutional meaning, one I explore mostly from James Madison's perspective in chapter 3. But the question of authority is vital and often overlooked in these conversations. One example, treated in detail in chapter 4, will suffice for the moment: Scholars like Hadley Arkes and Harry V. Jaffa make perceptive cases for understanding the Constitution in light of natural law and natural rights, especially as these are rooted in the Declaration of Independence. Yet this does not answer the indispensable question of *who* in the constitutional system is responsible for this application. The leap from this question to the frequent answer—judges—releases other constitutional actors, especially Congress and its constituents, from such a responsibility. It can only be recovered if, as Stoner notes, "Americans are willing to take responsibility for the Constitution themselves, or give political authority to elected leaders willing to take responsibility in their name."[6]

Republican constitutionalism assumes that natural-law arguments, like other arguments about constitutional meaning, are, or ought to be, ultimately political arguments. There is something deeply noble in habituating a republican people to the consideration of such important questions. The contemporary ethic is to outsource this function to judges, who are variously thought by their independence from election or their legal training to be uniquely and exclusively competent to deal with questions of justice, natural law, the proper scope of government, and even, in some inescapable cases, the prudence of laws. Yet the problem with their insulation from electoral politics is better stated as allowing the people's representatives to escape from responsibility for constitutional questions, as though their job was to make policy judgments based on their preferences and the function of judges was to police them. Legal training, moreover, is rigorous but rarely rooted anymore in questions of justice or natural law. It is not the jurisprudence of Edmund Burke, which contained the "collected reason of ages," but rather a techne that, as Burke is also said to have put it, "sharpens the mind by narrowing it."

What we need instead is an enlargement of the res publica, the space allocated to political conversation and a shared pursuit of common things. That is not the whole of political life, which involves the mundane as well as and probably more often than the noble. But the fact that we posit laws together helps make them constitutive of a particular political community. This legal positivism decidedly does not mean laws should have no moral content. All manner of laws have moral content that is ennobled, not undermined, by their having been written down and agreed to. Positivism is a claim about authority: who posits the law, and how. I hope to demonstrate that the best answer—in fact, the *moral* answer, the answer best in accord with the natural right to self-government—is a people placed in conditions that encourage deliberation and acting through representatives.

Finally, a note about the scholars whose view of constitutional authority I critique in the chapters that follow: One does not lightly enter a ring in which the formidable likes of Randy Barnett and Hadley Arkes await. They are among the preeminent constitutional theorists of our time. I hope they will take the study that follows, and the fact that their views merit extended treatment even if by way of disagreement, as a mark of esteem.

1. A Republican Constitution

> Now that there is reason to hope for the imminent demise of left-liberal activism by the Supreme Court, we must ask what our real objection was to the era that seems to be passing. Did we think that the illegitimacy of the Court's performance lay in its liberalism or in its activism, its politics or its contempt for law? Having endured for half a century a Court that seized authority not confided to it to lay down as unalterable law a liberal social agenda nowhere to be found in the actual Constitution of the United States, conservatives must decide whether they want a Court that behaves in the same way but in the service of their agenda.
>
> —Robert Bork[1]

President Obama was two-thirds of the way through his 2010 State of the Union address when he delivered the line that would have stunned the Founders: "With all due deference to the separation of powers," he averred, "last week, the Supreme Court reversed a century of law that I believe will open the floodgates for special interests, including foreign corporations, to spend without limit in our elections."[2] The reference was to *Citizens United v. Federal Election Commission,* in which the high court had ruled just a few days before that those who organized in the corporate form retained the right to spend on political causes.[3] The scene that ensued was, from the perspective of contemporary constitutional norms, awkward, perhaps even demagogic if not simply discourteous. The six justices of the Supreme Court who attended sat steps from the president's dais, expressionless, as Democratic members of Congress, some to the judges' immediate rear, erupted in cheers. The justices were a captive audience, inhibited by the conventions of judicial propriety from self-defense. Cameras captured Justice Samuel Alito apparently mouthing the words "not true."

Editorialists were aghast at this public display of conflict between a president and the Court, some because the president instigated it, others because a justice seemed to reply. A headline in the *New York Times* blared breathlessly, "Supreme Court Gets a Rare Rebuke, in Front of a Nation."[4] There was, of course, something inherently askew: the justices were constrained to silence amid hooting and hollering that approached the raucous atmosphere of a political rally. It was arguably unfair to criticize the judges in person in a forum in which propriety impeded a response, and the claim that *Citizens United* allowed foreign spending in elections was dubious at best.

Still, the line that would have puzzled President Obama's predecessor James Madison was not the critique of the Court but rather the apology with which it was introduced: "With all due deference to the separation of powers . . ." Actually, the separation of powers as Madison theorized it thrives on institutional combat. *Federalist* no. 51 announces this clearly in one of its most famous formulations: the separation of powers is maintained by "giving to those who administer each department, the necessary constitutional means, and personal motives, to resist encroachments of the others. . . . Ambition must be made to counteract ambition."[5] The Supreme Court may once have been "the least dangerous"[6] branch of government, but today, commanding widespread deference to its rulings, it is hardly a flickering flame that needs protection from the howling winds of constitutional politics. Perhaps those politics were demagogically executed in this instance. But the justices were surely not the hapless, powerless victims they were made out to be.

THE REPUBLICAN CONSTITUTION VS.
THE INDIVIDUALIST CONSTITUTION

This is a book about why the judiciary should be subject to the normal operation of the separation of powers and why constitutional conflict that involves the courts is politically healthy. The case is neither that every issue should be decided politically, nor that the Supreme Court should never act. Rather, the chapters that follow attempt to ground the justification for and practice of originalism in what I shall call "republican constitutionalism." The grounding consists of the classical goods of political activity and obligation, of which excessive judicial interference with politics deprives us. The practice is the people's authority and responsibility to participate through their elected representatives in the process of constitutional interpretation. Under a regime of republican constitutionalism, judicial modesty would be admirable but not assumed. The elected branches would check judges when they veer outside their duty to interpret the clear words and original understanding of the Constitution: in other words, when they refuse to void only those acts of the political branches that are, in Alexander Hamilton's formulation, at "irreconcilable variance" between statutory and fundamental law.[7] Moreover, republican constitutionalism sees the judiciary as having the most authority under cases clearly within its ambit—say, the definition of a jury or the rights of criminal defendants—and the least in cases of conflict between the other branches. The Supreme Court would be regarded not as the independent and ultimate umpire of the regime but rather as a player within it, one with a vital role but also one that should itself be brushed back if it crowds the constitutional plate.

It is "republican" insofar as it leaves room for the res publica, the "public thing," the vital area of public activity that connects individuals to the larger political community. Jeremy Waldron has argued that republicanism is based on "the idea of 'the citizen.' The idea of the citizen is not the idea of a political specialist, and it does not simply expand or contract its meaning according to a user's views about how political authority should be distributed. The idea of the citizen is in the first instance the idea of an ordinary full member of the society—a member of the public whose affairs are properly comprised in the res publica."[8] Republican constitutionalism similarly rejects what Benjamin Kleinerman has called a "profoundly antipolitical conception of the Madisonian constitutional order" evident in contemporary liberalism.[9] The notion of constitutionalism articulated in these pages is also "republican" because it assumes that public activity must be "refine[d] and enlarge[d]," as *Federalist* no. 10 explains, through the medium of elected representatives. Those representatives, too, would participate in constitutional deliberation and the shaping of constitutional meaning. They would be accountable to the public but operate at a step of remove from it.

Republican constitutionalism is given vitality by ongoing contestation and a sense of commitment and devotion by a political community that sees itself as sharing certain ends. Of course, communities are diverse and their politics can be ugly. But the ends can be thin, and that diversity should serve to moderate majorities by forcing them to compromise in order to prevail. They should leave ample space for individual choice; liberty itself should be one of the ends we share. But they should also recognize that human beings living in society share physical and moral space with one another and that one admirable and indispensable virtue is tailoring and, where necessary, trimming our behavior, appetites, and ends to public goods and others' needs. Such a virtue goes by various names. On a grand scale, it is patriotism; day to day, we call it civility. If political life so modestly conceived—not one that requires a reconstruction of communities or a wholesale reeducation of citizens, but rather one that simply recognizes some degree of public goods and common space—is impossible, so is republican government. Republican constitutionalism does not require philosophers; it requires citizens. Equally important: if the people are too corrupt to govern themselves, there is no reason to believe judges drawn from the same source will do better; if anything, their insulation from the community may entrench their own prejudices.

Republican constitutionalism entails, inherently, some recognition of the transgenerational authority of a political tradition and community. Political communities are not good at many things, and as such ought to be limited in their power and scope. But as expressions of shared purpose, they can be both vital and decent. As opportunities for the practice of public virtues, they can be irreplaceable. That does not mean they are the only or even the primary space for virtue—one can help an elderly person across the street without a command from the state—but it is to say they can be noble spaces.

Republican constitutionalism preserves an appropriate distance between the immediate and the deliberate rule of the community. The term "republican," as opposed to Larry D. Kramer's "popular constitutionalism," which "assign[s] ordinary citizens a central and pivotal role in implementing their Constitution,"[10] denotes both this distance and its grounding in both classical politics and transgenerational obligation. Kramer writes: "[I]f neither judges nor legislators were responsible for interpreting and enforcing fundamental law, who was? The people themselves."[11] This denial that legislators are responsible for constitutional interpretation, as well as Kramer's examples of early Americans acting through jury decisions and popular demonstrations, suggests an immediacy republican constitutionalism would discourage. Rather, republican constitutionalism shares more in common with James W. Ceaser's "political constitution," which is composed not of legal rules but rather of political judgments.[12] Republican constitutionalism also differs fundamentally from Randy E. Barnett's "Republican Constitution," which is actually an *individualist* constitution and, moreover, a *presentist* one. That is, its authority is drawn from our choices in the here and now. For Barnett, a "republican" constitution differs from a "democratic" constitution according to the location of sovereignty: "What separates a Republican Constitution from a Democratic Constitution is its conception of 'popular sovereignty.' Where a Democratic Constitution views sovereignty as residing in the people collectively or as a group, a Republican Constitution views sovereignty as residing in the people as individuals."[13]

On Barnett's reading, the essence of a Republican Constitution is that rights precede government. This is a rebuttal of legal positivism; the problem is that its dichotomy is too stark. People do retain rights when they form government, but on Locke's account they trade the rights of the state of nature for *civil* rights: rights associated with citizenship that are regulable by the community. Their purposes are limited by the most important feature of a civil right: its direction toward the common good. Locke describes the exchange:

> But though men when they enter into society give up the equality, liberty, and executive power they had in the state of Nature into

the hands of the society, to be so far disposed of by the legislative as the good of the society shall require, yet it being only with an intention in every one the better to preserve himself, his liberty and property (for no rational creature can be supposed to change his condition with an intention to be worse), the power of the society or legislative constituted by them can never be supposed to extend farther than the common good, but is obliged to secure every one's property by providing against those three defects above mentioned that made the state of Nature so unsafe and uneasy.[14]

As an act of citizens, the Constitution is best understood not simply as positive law or solely as natural law but rather as fundamental law. Some distinctions are essential. First, while the Constitution may be rooted in natural law, it is an *act* of positive law. The positing of law matters not because it is always right, but rather because it is a political act that helps to constitute a particular rather than a cosmopolitan political community. Second, while it is an act of positive law, it is also one of *fundamental* law that outranks other—that is, statutory—forms of positive law. Third, the interpretive authority of judges arises from and thus is limited to the Constitution's status as (explicitly written) positive rather than natural law; that is, the power of judicial review extends to the reconciliation of two conflicting acts of positive law, one fundamental and the other statutory. Thus *Federalist* no. 78: "A constitution is in fact, and must be, regarded by the judges as a fundamental law" with "superior obligation and validity" to statutory law because it emanates from "the people" rather than "their agents." Note that Publius makes no claim for a natural-law authority of the Constitution: Both constitutional and statutory law are human artifices. One trumps the other because it emanates more fundamentally from the people. Note that in *Federalist* no. 78 judges are not protecting minorities from majorities but rather "the people"—understood, significantly, as a whole; that is, as a political community—from the depositories of power: "their agents." The courts consequently serve "as an intermediate body between the people and the legislature."[15] It is law that is ratified—posited—by the people and is, as

Federalist no. 53 says, "unalterable by the government."[16] It is insufficient simply to say that rights precede government, for that does not answer the question of how they are to be defined and regulated and, more important, *who* is to do the defining and regulating.

Barnett's Constitution, like that of most proponents of judicial engagement, is also "presentist" insofar as it assumes legitimacy is measured in discrete and immediate moments. Barnett writes that the "consent of the people" would have to be unanimous to escape being a fiction. Instead, he argues that the individual is bound in conscience to the Constitution by its guarantee of passing only "necessary and proper" laws that protect individual rights. The important fact is the temporal framework. The individual's obligation to the regime is up for grabs at any given moment in the present. That the Constitution is customary cannot bind us; only its persuasiveness now can.

For Barnett, a "republican constitution" is one that protects individuals, whereas a "democratic constitution" empowers the people as a whole.[17] Yet this miscasts the terms of the Madisonian distinction between democracy and republicanism, which pertained not to where sovereignty resided but rather to how it was expressed. While it is true that the Framers were concerned about *immediate* majority rule, it is equally true that their aim was to institutionalize *deliberate* majority rule. In this sense, Barnett's reinterpretation of republicanism would have surprised Madison. When Madison referred to the "republican principle" in *Federalist* no. 10, he explicitly meant majority rule. He called majority rule "the vital principle of our free Constitution."[18] He similarly wrote that "the vital principle of republican government is the *lex majoris partis,* the will of the majority."[19]

THE RISE OF JUDICIAL ENGAGEMENT

The context of this book is the rising influence among constitutional conservatives of the theory of judicial engagement—the belief that judges should, as Adam J. White puts it, "put government on trial," removing the longstanding presumption of constitutionality in favor of what Barnett, among the most distinguished advocates of the theory, calls a "presumption of liberty" that would force government to demonstrate that legislation is rational and necessary.[20] This is said to protect the individual against the government, but it also applies—a very different scenario, as we shall see in chapter 3—to instances of majority-minority conflict, and thus is a means of restricting political community. One of judicial engagement's foremost proponents, Clark M. Neily III, describes it this way: "Judicial engagement means deciding cases on the basis of actual facts, without bent or bias in favor of government. It means ensuring that the government has a valid reason for restricting people's freedom and that it exercises that power with at least a modicum of care. It means not turning a blind eye when government pursues constitutionally illegitimate ends."[21]

But judicial engagement means more than this, which Neily does not deny: it means not merely that legislatures and executives should deliberate and check each other, but rather that judges should have the final say in these matters. They are robed guardians on whom we ultimately rely for protection. Notice, however, a theme to which we shall return: on the theory of judicial engagement, it is always the government against the individual, never the community against individuals. In other words, individuals assert their rights against the government, which appears as a foreign entity, somehow divorced from the people who elected it. There is no right for the community to govern itself in accord with its values, only the right of the individual person—not "the people" in their corporate capacity"—to be exempt. Neily understands the entire purpose of the Constitution—a document forged precisely because the "government" of the Articles of Confederation was impotent and unable to accomplish its ends—to be to inhibit government action:

> Why do we have a constitution at all? Why not Athenian-style direct democracy or a representative government with the power to do whatever politicians think best? Very simply, it's because

government is not your friend. It is not your mother, your father, or a benevolent uncle. Nor is it your partner, your colleague, or your teammate. As far as the government is concerned, it is your boss, setting policies and issuing edicts that you will obey. Between that awesome power and you stands the Constitution.[22]

There is something to this. Government can of course get out of control, and *The Federalist* provides a solution for the problem, which is the separation of powers: the tension between all three branches, not just judicial decree.

But Neily's simplified theory entirely divests the political community not just of the ability to act in prescribed areas but also of its responsibility for confining its decisions to those areas. The government is indeed not your friend, relative, or partner. But in a certain sense it is *you*, an entity the community elects and whose preferences ultimately command it. The American regime is not the Athenian polis, but neither is it wholly modern. As Francis Slade observes, it is characteristic of the modern conception of politics for the sovereign—which is reason—to stand above the community ruling it.[23] But this is not the American system, which occupies a constructive space bridging the classical and the modern. In this space, politics is the process by which a community acts on its values, which include liberty but may in some places include limits. The nation is allowed to make these decisions where the Constitution authorizes them, and localities are empowered to do so except where the Constitution specifically forbids them. On Neily's account, we have not merely a government but a *people* out of control, and thus we need judges to discipline not simply an extraneous object called "the government" but also our neighbors.

Under the theory of judicial engagement, judges should not be reluctant to interfere with operations of the elected branches of government: They should, instead, see themselves as coequal partners in governing and should therefore lean forward and assert themselves, especially on behalf of the individual. On some versions of this approach, government would bear the burden in all cases to prove *to judges* the necessity and propriety of its acts. The disagreement among constitutional conservatives thus consists of both the tools judges use and their disposition while using them. But it should consist equally of the tools available to the elected branches to counteract judges, tools they have largely abandoned.

The fundamental problem with judicial engagement is that the individual it aims to shield from majority rule is situated in a political context. We share space, both literally and metaphorically, with other people in overlapping political communities, and the range of things we do that actually affect only ourselves is almost vanishingly thin. Conservatism not always but generally has held that the rest should be lightly governed, but also that they should be governed by the people rather than by elites. William F. Buckley famously said that he would rather be governed by the first 2,000 people in the Boston telephone directory than by the first 2,000 members of the Harvard faculty. Aristotle recognized the wisdom of crowds, and Edmund Burke understood custom and tradition as the accumulation of wisdom over time. Yet judicial engagement, in the name of a technocratic and antiseptic understanding of rationality that bears greater relation to the Progressive aspiration to "scientific legislation" than to the conservative understanding of the nobility of politics, would transfer broad swaths of authority from the people over time to the first nine members of the federal judiciary right now.

Tocqueville recognized that the desiccation of the res publica, the space between individuals and the state, creates the conditions for tyranny. Aristotle likewise said the tyrant seeks to eliminate layers of common endeavor between himself and the tyrannized. More recently, the sociologist Robert Nisbet made similar observations, noting that human beings are political and that they will seek community in the state if they are otherwise isolated from one another.[24] That it is the tyranny of the learned—that is, judges, who overwhelmingly are indeed well educated—is little comfort, and may be particular aggravation, for the tyrannized. Tyranny is not too strong a word. James Madison said in *Federalist* no. 47 that the conjunction of the legislative with the judicial power would constitute exactly that—tyranny—and it is a condition in which judicial engagement substantially places us. To be sure, judicial engagement far more impedes than compels policy, but the inhibition of policy—saying "no" to this idea or that—is also a legislative function. Indeed, the fact that judicial engagement sees judicial duty almost exclusively as a tool for stopping political activity itself suggests that it is an attempt to read John Stuart Mill's "harm principle," according to which coercive authority is only justified to prevent harm of one person by another, into the Constitution.

THE CLAIMS OF COMMUNITY

Judicial engagement, of course, sees tyranny differently—much as Robert A. Dahl did, as the "severe deprivation of a natural right,"[25] a case in which, proponents of this view hold, the judge is duty bound to intercede to protect individuals against the community or, depending on the theorist in question, against legislators purporting to act in the name of the community. To libertarian devotees of the theory, it consists primarily of courts telling the government it cannot act.

But just as individuals have claims against the community, so does the community have claims on individuals. It is a political virtue to suppress personal appetites for the sake of the public good, but it is also a discharge of a debt. When Socrates's friend Crito, in the Platonic dialogue bearing the latter's name, offers the great philosopher a chance to escape his date with hemlock, Socrates declines. His obligation to the political community in return for what it has given to him—he was born to parents married under the laws of Athens, was educated according to those laws, was himself married and had children under Athenian laws to whose authority he has never objected—would make it unjust for him to destroy the city by undermining the authority of its government. Socrates imagines a conversation in which the laws of Athens challenge him as to who owes whom the superior obligation. Athenians are free, the laws explain, to persuade the community at any point at which they find the regime unjust, and to leave it if they fail.

But we claim that whoever of you stays behind, and can see the way we judge cases in court and otherwise govern the city, has made an agreement with us, by staying and not leaving, that he'll do whatever we order him to do; and we claim that anyone who doesn't obey us is guilty of injustice in three ways: first, that he's not obeying us when we are his progenitors; second, that he is not obeying us when we brought him up; and third, that having made an agreement with us to obey our instructions, he is neither obeying us, nor persuading us if there's anything amiss in what we're doing.[26]

We are, of course, a very great distance in modernity from Socrates's conception of all-embracing laws according to which one's parents' marriage creates an obligation to submit to a death sentence. The overly literal reader of Socrates might conclude he supports an all-powerful regime, even a totalitarian one, whose any act is legitimate and whose every decision deserves accession. But Socrates rarely spoke for the literal minded. We do not owe the regime everything; nor is it responsible for everything: citizens constitute *both* a community *and* individuals. Socrates wrote prior to the modern separation between the public and private. Still, as a metaphor for political obligation, the *Crito* is a compelling reminder that living together is a bargain in which not every individual can have everything he or she wants while also maintaining the good of the whole, and that the integrity of the whole benefits each of us as individuals. The concept of tacit consent that Socrates foresees, and which later emerges more explicitly in the *Second Treatise* of John Locke, is itself questionable. Despite the fact that some celebrity members of the losing party invariably entertain the polity with threats to move abroad after an unfavorable presidential election, they almost never do and, more important, most citizens have no such realistic option in the first place.

But explicit, temporal consent is also a mirage. There is no moment at which we can all exercise it, and no theory that can command universal assent unless our highest human good is to be left alone, which is to say if our noblest ambition is loneliness. The French political thinker Bertrand de Jouvenel wrote that, as Daniel J. Mahoney has summarized it, "man's liberty and dignity depend upon a gracious acceptance of his status as a dependent being."[27] Dependence is not our choice; it is our natural condition and, indeed, a natural gift. Burke described the mysterious primacy of feeling over rational choice in creating obligation: "Dark and inscrutable are the ways by which we come into the world. The instincts which give rise to this mysterious process of nature are not of our making. But out of physical causes, unknown to us, perhaps unknowable, arise moral duties, which, as we are able perfectly to comprehend, we are bound indispensably to perform."[28] The obligations of parents to children and children to parents are of this variety. So is our obligation to the political community.

The difference here is largely one of political theory, not merely constitutional law. Barnett denies that "We the People" exists as "an entity capable of making decisions, reaching judgments, having a will, and 'changing their mind.'"[29] On his understanding, the phrase refers instead to all individuals.[30] But this is not how politics works. The political community does exist, and as we shall see that Aristotle suggested, it exists ontologically as something that transcends individuals. That can be a dangerous concept in the wrong hands, just as an overly stringent understanding of individual rights can trigger a collapse of common endeavor and moral consensus. It is, as I shall argue, all the more reason to revive a robust federalism that makes local political activity meaningful. But there is an important observation to be made. The claim of isolated individuals each free to evaluate their obligation to the community is rationalistic to the core. It is the voice of reason enchanted with itself and unaware of its own limitations. It is also the voice of the individual intoxicated with his own freedom and unwilling to accept boundaries or duties.

Barnett declares that consent of the governed cannot serve as a normative model for construing the Constitution because not every individual has consented to it. He does not, of course, mean a literal process of door-to-door unanimous consent. He means that to command our legitimate obedience, the regime must restrict itself to the constitutional standard of laws that are necessary and proper, with legal—which is to say judicial—assurances made to the citizen.[31] Yet this conclusion about the consent of the governed—that is, Barnett's claim that it is a fiction unless it is unanimous—contains its premise: its reasoning presupposes an individualist ethos the Founding generation did not share. Without it, the statement unwinds, or rather tangles, into tautology: the consent of the governed means the consent of every individual because that is what consent of the governed means. It did not mean that to the Founders, which raises claims about this approach's entitlement to the label "originalism." When the Founders objected in the Declaration of Independence to being taxed or forced to shelter soldiers without their consent, they meant consent by popularly elected legislatures in which majorities bound minorities. But the converse of this is also true. They meant the majority could bind political minorities by law.

A POLITICAL CASE AGAINST JUDICIAL SUPREMACY

Under the activism of the Warren Court, judicial conservatives shared an understanding that the space for the judge was confined by the far larger authority of the political branches, while it was generally liberals who sought an active judiciary. Relatively recently, constitutional conservatives considered the late Judge Robert Bork, denied confirmation to the Supreme Court in a 1987 debate in which his views were wildly distorted, to be a martyr. But now the sides have, at least in many circles, switched. Liberals like Mark Tushnet are among the foremost advocates of judicial restraint, while judicial engagement has made Bork, in growing circles on the legal right, into a pariah.[32] Bork's position, elucidated repeatedly, was legal positivism, but we are mistaken if we take that, as many of his critics do, as a synonym for moral relativism and a cascade of other evils. Bork meant simply that law is what we posit it to be. He did not mean our choices as to laws were normless—on the contrary, he noted that "all law is based upon moral judgments"—or that all laws were morally equivalent to each other, only that the office of a judge is to apply positive law.[33]

Bork's point is one of the authority to impose philosophical views of government, not of whether they exist. In an often though rarely completely quoted passage, he writes: "There is no way of deciding [moral] matters other than by reference to some system of moral or ethical values that has no objective or intrinsic validity of its own and about which men can and do differ." But Bork immediately proceeds to explain himself: "Where the Constitution does not embody the moral or ethical choice, the judge has no basis other than *his own* values upon which to set aside the community judgment embodied in the statute."[34] That is, "his own" view as opposed to that of the people's elected representatives. Bork's position that the judge should be confined to applying positive law rather than imposing canons of natural law or rights that exceed the language of the Constitution and consequently provide too much ambit and temptation to jurists is now commonly pilloried on the legal right.

In a sense, this book is a case for Bork and against engagement, but it is not simply that. It is a case against judicial supremacy, but not simply for judicial restraint. Restraint is a disposition in search of a theory. Proponents of restraint, few of whom want to abolish judicial review, are often reduced to saying they favor restraint except when they favor a decision. So while restraint's most distinguished contemporary exponent, Judge J. Harvie Wilkinson III,[35] has called it an antitheory, it also needs more than a tendency. Without a political grounding, judicial restraint is vulnerable to the complaint Tara Smith levels against minimalism: that its "hollowness at the core" emphasizes the degree of the activity over its content.[36]

The need is less to advocate judicial restraint than to articulate the place constitutional conservatism sees the judiciary occupying within a system of separated powers. While it is a myth that the competitive apparatus of separation of powers assumes each branch will unreservedly pursue its powers to the hilt, neither the executive nor the legislative department is expected to regard exclusive self-restraint as its modus operandi. We expect the Congress and president to make a good-faith effort to enact those laws and policies they view as constitutional, but they are not merely trusted to do so. Yet neither are their decisions, once made, given the blind deference it is broadly assumed the judiciary is owed. Rather, with regard to executive and legislative decisions, all three branches are understood to embrace one another in an ongoing constitutional dance. As John Agresto notes, exempting the judiciary from this conflict would make it, no less than the other branches, an absolute power.[37]

Republican constitutionalism is, I shall contend, what the Framers envisioned, but my purpose is also to establish the idea that a regime in which the Constitution is a political document—one that binds by obligation and the goods of political life—is normatively best for its citizens and for its own health. That is, this book makes a *political* case for a judiciary subjected to the separation of powers. This may seem a contradiction in terms. We are accustomed to assuming that politics and constitutionalism occupy separate realms, with the latter governing the former. Kramer has written of the Founding era:

> Reconciling the existence in the eighteenth century of a constitution that was "law" with the absence of any notion that judges had a special role in determining its meaning has proved difficult for modern minds to grasp. In our world, there is law and there is politics, with nothing much in between. For us, the Constitution is a subset of law, and law is something presumptively and primarily, even if not exclusively, within the province of courts.[38]

Yet, as Kramer also argues, majorities can and ought to be involved in constitutional politics, properly understood.

RECOVERING THE GOODS OF POLITICS

"Politics" has acquired a sordid, tawdry cast associated with raw power or the selfish pursuit of egoistic preferences. It was not so to the ancients. When Aristotle taught that "man is a political animal," he meant not that we were power-hungry or prone to domination or voracious consumers of opinion polls and cable news. Rather, his point was the simple fact, familiar to any self-reflective person, of our interdependence, our inability to flourish without one another. Of course, the Greek city-state is long gone, and the republican glories of civic Rome are romanticized in our memories. To ground a case for originalism and the behavior of judges in classical politics is to administer a highly diluted tonic, but one made from strong medicine. The city is gone as a literal entity, but the idea of politics as a means of pursuing human goods through interdependent life survives, or can. That does not mean the imposition of a rigid and thick code of morality from on high; on the contrary, the intent in these pages is to prevent judges from doing precisely that. It does mean an openness to shared ideas of noble ends pursued with common purpose.

I mean something different here than what Justice Stephen Breyer has called "active liberty," a rule by which the Constitution should be construed according to its democratic character. Breyer, following Benjamin Constant, admirably distinguishes between ancient liberty, which encompassed the duty to participate in politics, and modern liberty, which is concerned with the protection of the individual. But while Breyer calls for judicial restraint, allowing judges to define democracy is itself to assign to them an immense and inescapably active power. Breyer, for example, would view campaign finance not just from the point of view of protecting speech, an explicit First Amendment objective, but also from the point of view of "promotion of a democratic conversation." The authority to define what promotes democratic conversation and what does not inescapably entails interfering in the democratic process.

Consider Breyer's standard of review: "Courts can defer to the legislature's own judgment insofar as that judgment concerns matters (particularly empirical matters) about which the legislature is comparatively expert, such as the extent of the campaign finance problem, a matter that directly concerns the realities of political life. But courts should not defer when they evaluate the risk that reform legislation will defeat the participatory self-government objective itself."[39] Judges, for Breyer as for John Hart Ely, are the arbiters of what democracy means.[40] This is not, then, a theory that restricts judicial authority: it is a normative, and consequentialist, claim for how judges should use the extensive authority they are purported to have. In this sense, it is of the same breed as judicial engagement: the difference is the terms—ancient or modern—on which judges should engage. Republican constitutionalism would simply allow political processes to play out, and permit the liberty of the ancients to assert itself as having a place amid the important contours provided by the liberty of the moderns, by not allocating judges unchecked power. Excessive judicial activity crowds out political activity even when its goal is to encourage it.

The Framers were comfortable in the space linking the liberty of the ancients and that of the moderns—a space that thinks of the people as both individuals and as a political community. The point is evident in Thomas Jefferson's famous letter explaining that the Declaration of Independence arose from the "harmonizing sentiments of the day, whether expressed in conversation, in letters, printed essays, or in the elementary books of public right, as Aristotle, Cicero, Locke, Sidney, &c."[41] That "public" in "public right" is suggestive, as is Jefferson's collapsing of the ancients and moderns into a single concatenation of "harmoniz[ed]" influences. The tendency today, rather, is to consider Locke to be the prophet of the individual's ascendance over the community, and thus a radical break from Aristotle. Yet consider the subtlety in the declaration's assignment of "unalienable rights" that are mostly alienable—that is, able to be transferred in exchange for an equivalent—by individuals. Indeed, alienating one's individual right to liberty is the entire basis of Lockean political society. One alienates it in exchange for civil rights that Locke explicitly says are subject to the decisions of the majority. The declaration's rights make sense only as the unalienable rights of the American people to self-government. This reading is reinforced by the much-overlooked bill of particulars against King George III, who was largely accused of violating the colonists' right to govern themselves as a political community. The declaration's preamble appeals to the abstract rights of all men, but its complaints render that commitment concrete in protesting violations of the particular rights of Englishmen.

Somewhere between there and here, politics became a symbol not of dignity but of imposition, corruption, or both. Of course, assailing politicians is an American pastime, but outright contempt for politics has not always been, and the perversion of the word itself makes the recovery of a republican Constitution difficult.

THE PARADOX OF ENGAGEMENT

Genuinely republican constitutionalism requires several other preconditions, including many from which we have fallen away. Some of these are institutional, but the most important is attitudinal. We must overcome our reflexive distaste for politics. Among the public at large, this takes the form of a discomfort with conflict. When the branches of government clash, which Madison tells us they are supposed to do, we see dysfunction. When a president criticizes the Supreme Court and a justice replies, we claim impropriety. When members of Congress disagree with each other, we cry gridlock, call it bickering, and complain that they are "unproductive."

The reality is that all these are signs of constitutional health. As George Thomas has put it, a Madisonian Constitution that embraces the people's "responsibility for constitutional judgments" rather than judicial supremacy might make us "more comfortable as a polity with constitutional quarrels" and thus "more appreciative of constitutional forms."[42] This book seeks to reclaim them for politics nobly understood. The alternative is a technocratic division of labor according to which questions of a constitutional character, or at least final authority over them, is assigned to judges on account of their particular expertise and presumed neutrality. This has become the dominant paradigm in American constitutional thought, such that the question now is not whether judges have authority in a given area but rather how assertive they should be in using it.

Giving judges the final word—making them "supreme in the exposition of the law of the Constitution," in the noted and self-aggrandizing formulation of *Cooper v. Aaron*[43]—raises serious questions of exactly the kind that most concern advocates of judicial engagement: namely, those pertaining to liberty. A judge with final authority over the Constitution might expand personal liberty, but might also contract it; and the record of the judiciary in this area is decidedly mixed compared to that of Congress, which arguably has done more practical good in the expansion of rights than the courts.[44] The judiciary is a fragile basket in which to place every constitutional egg, especially for those who hold to the premise that government—of which judges are a part—is infinitely power-hungry and forever straining at its bit. It is generally a good rule of constitutional thumb never to trust a friend with a power one would not want transferred, as it always and inevitably will be, to an adversary.

The relevant question is how, especially according to the political thought of the Founding generation, we should *expect* judges whose power is uncontested to behave. Judges are political actors, after all; which is not to say they throw caution to the constitutional winds, but rather to note they are human beings with power and are subject to the normal motivations and infirmities of other human beings so situated. The Anti-Federalist writer Brutus was wrong about a great deal, but he had the Constitution dead to rights on this. Judges with absolute power not only *might* behave poorly, he warned, they would be especially *prone* to. There would be no appeal from the rulings of the Supreme Court, he observed, and that would affect the dispositions of its judges: "In short, [the justices of the Supreme Court] are independent of the people, of the legislature, and of every power under heaven. Men placed in this situation will generally soon feel themselves independent of heaven itself."

Today the judiciary is no longer the "least dangerous" branch of Hamilton's reassurances. The very trappings of office designed to fortify it with mystery and ceremony have contributed to a sense that the Constitution is a text of Talmudic complexity that cannot be understood unless a priesthood of lawyers and judges intervenes. Having been trained in the rigors of legal analysis and modes of thought, this priesthood is thought to be uniquely qualified to dispense justice and safeguard rights. Perhaps that is so; perhaps, in other senses, it cramps their perspective to the exclusion of politics. In either case, the perspective according to which a charter of government would be so complex in its meaning as to be inaccessible to its citizens, requiring the intervention of professional interpreters, raises questions about the legitimacy of the individual consent on which some forms of libertarian constitutionalism so depend. Christopher Wolfe explains: "It would be inappropriate for the framework of a democratic republic to be or become a species of technical knowledge, since the average citizen of a democracy is presumed to have the requisite knowledge to participate in his or her own government, and knowledge of the fundamental law is perhaps the fundamental knowledge on which a citizen's actions must be based."[45]

Moreover, even were judges wiser and better positioned to safeguard rights, the possibility that this very status might create temptations to abuse their protective power seems largely to escape the notice of a legal theory that, being suspicious of every other governmental actor, in many dimensions distills to this: because no one can be trusted with unchecked power, judges must be trusted with unchecked power. The linear model of constitutionalism, according to which laws leave the station at Congress, stop next at the White House, and ultimately disembark at the judiciary—the model of *Cooper v. Aaron*—does precisely that, which is to say precisely what Brutus feared.

We may think of this as the "Paradox of Engagement": advocates of judicial engagement do not trust people with power; hence the need for judges to check them. But the foundations of their theory are laid on a breathtaking faith in *judges'* ability to reason correctly—though the advocates themselves do not agree on what conclusions they would reach—and to resist the temptations of power. Consider two passages from Timothy Sandefur, a libertarian proponent of judicial engagement: "People are fallible, with personal biases and imperfect knowledge, incapable of precisely weighing other people's priorities or making good decisions for them. Attempting to do so clashes with each person's moral responsibility and independent judgment."[46] Yet, in a formulation that recalls the old saw about the economist in a pit who assumes a ladder in order to escape, he also declares: "Judges can misunderstand or misapply legal theories, or even abuse them to reach corrupt decisions. But that is an argument for choosing judges carefully—not an argument for discarding the law itself."[47] In other words, assume a principled judge.

The paradox is that the fallibility of people in the first sentence necessitates the engagement of judges—who are, after all, people, not demigods—in the second. There is also a substantial difference between rejecting judicial supremacy and "discarding the law." More important, in this more than anything, Sandefur discloses the incompatibility of judicial engagement with the Framers' constitutionalism. Madison warned in *Federalist* no. 51 that constitutional architecture was necessary because men were not angels and angels did not govern men. To give judges extensive powers on the mere hope they will, first, be chosen carefully and, second, remain faithful to their trust is wholly un-Madisonian.

JUDGES AS GUARDIANS

More troubling still is this: What if all judges were wise and all political questions had determinate answers that were objectively wrong or right? Would we, on these premises, want to live in a society in which authority was transferred to them? Readers of Plato will recognize these as superficial likenesses of the philosopher-kings of his *Republic.* But Aristotelians, knowing men as political animals, will also recognize this society as impoverished in a meaningful way, deprived of some of the most basic human activity. Its citizens will have been relieved of what Tocqueville called "the trouble of thinking and the pain of living."[48] Judge Learned Hand famously put the issue in Platonic terms: "For myself it would be most irksome to be ruled by a bevy of Platonic Guardians, even if I knew how to choose them, which I assuredly do not. If they were in charge, I should miss the stimulus of living in a society where I have, at least theoretically, some part in the direction of public affairs."[49]

Citizens so ruled will not have been deprived of all choices, to be sure, for not all choices are political; indeed, some of our most important choices are not. But the public deliberation of consequential things that concern matters outside ourselves nonetheless fills a human need whose emptiness would otherwise allow individualism to consume us. As Tocqueville reminds us, concern with the public weal draws us across the moats we otherwise build around ourselves amid conditions of equality and independence. To deprive us of the ability to act on our Aristotelian natures in the name of a judicial technocracy is to deprive us of something deeply and uniquely human. And when not exercised, these capacities of self-government atrophy, reinforcing the cycle of judicial supremacy from the inside.

Defenders of judicial engagement rooted in individual rights protest that they are not proposing giving political authority, only constitutional authority, to judges. That is, judges would determine the boundaries of political authority, not the content of political decisions. Even presuming, which is questionable, that these questions can be neatly separated, this is immense authority that advocates of an assertive judiciary often simply assume, without supporting argument, is exclusively judicial in nature. Yet the Constitution nowhere assumes this; nor did those who framed it.

Of course, no one is suggesting that all authority be transferred to judges. But a growing chorus on both left and right asserts, though on different issues, that judges should be empowered to remove a burgeoning swath of issues from the public realm and, importantly, to exercise unchecked authority in doing so. Even the authority to decide which these are is itself immense. But it also almost inevitably comes with the matching power to shape the contours of the residual authority majorities retain. And this is to say nothing of the fact that not all judges are wise, and not all political or constitutional questions have obvious or objective answers. Judicial engagement would have the judge to whom the Constitution does not supply a clear answer search for one, perhaps by means of "constitutional construction." The Constitution is indeed ambiguous on several points, but that ambiguity can be healthy; and where it is not, as Keith Whittington has argued, the task of construction is intrinsically political in nature.[50]

Proponents of judicial engagement assert they aim to *defend* a realm of choice by inhibiting the intrusion of the state into protected regions, whether it is, depending on their perspectives, the right to do as one wills with one's body or the right to do what one wishes with one's guns. But it is the privatization of choice, the calling card of modernity, that most aptly characterizes this argument. The classically political is expunged. It is a dicey business to speak of the views of a group as diverse as "the Framers" any more than to speak today of those of "the Congress," but it is reasonably safe to say that for the vast bulk of them the essential right was not individual but rather political. It was, as we shall see developed more specifically in the pages that follow, participation in the processes of self-government.[51]

Rather than a linear model that leaves judges unchecked, republican constitutionalism sees the Constitution's meaning being discerned through an ongoing conversation between all three branches of government, answerable, in an ultimate sense, to the people—in other words, politics, rightly understood. It places demands on all three branches of government to engage constitutionally. It defends a place for judicial review, but as a means of facilitating, in an ultimate sense, rather than impeding the mechanisms of self-government. It rejects the constitutional indolence or abdication of elected officials who decline to defend their authority on the grounds that, in one infamous formulation, "the Court will clean it up."[52]

Judicial engagement, by contrast, is left in the uncomfortable position of trusting power—namely, the power of judges. As we have seen, that it does so precisely because it does not trust power in other hands—legislators, majorities and so forth—makes the position all the more paradoxical. And the problems multiply. The judicial remedy advocates of engagement would administer can be just as easily dispensed by judges with whom they disagree. Engagement is as available to liberal judicial activists as to conservative ones. Untethering judicial review from explicit constitutionalism by seeing the Ninth Amendment as a font of unenumerated individual rights—as opposed to a rule of construction that underscores the enumerated nature of congressional power—makes it difficult for conservatives to provide a coherent explanation for why these include economic rights but not social ones.[53] That is an explanation many libertarian theorists, of course, are happy to supply, both because they value each right equally and perhaps because they see the courts as instruments simply for preventing government action. Substantive readings of the Due Process Clause of the Fourteenth Amendment that serve conservative causes suffer from the same difficulty. And an eagerness to override sweeping federal statutes enabled by electoral majorities, like the Affordable Care Act, makes the argument of deference less available when conservatives want to leave such issues as same-sex marriage or abortion to political processes.

The Framers nowhere endorsed the notion of engaged judges as the term is now used, and they several times indicated their opposition to it. That matters because we are *their* heirs, not either members of a universal human community or autonomous agents of free-ranging political choice. In *Federalist* no. 49, James Madison warned against too often attempting to replicate the "ticklish" experiment of founding.[54] To say, as Barnett does, that we are morally bound only by those laws that meet an immediate test of legitimacy—that is, one that satisfies us here and now, without reference to the authority of the past—is to make founding an eternal recurrence.[55] To travel "beyond the Constitution," in Hadley Arkes's formulation of a jurisprudence of natural law, is to forsake the particularity that makes politics possible and meaningful. To be sure, the politics of natural law is richer than the politics of individual freedom, and there is no question that the Founders were more generally situated in that milieu than we are today. But their commitment to natural law is reflected not in judicial imposition but rather in its use to guide the conscience of the community, whose political mechanisms would be constructed to encourage their compliance with it.

In either case, the Constitution's legitimacy arises not from isolated individual calculation but from our political natures and generational obligations. Originalism has been justified on grounds of popular sovereignty, but that does not explain why rule of the people is itself a good; and this case too suffers from a presentist understanding of the people's relation to the Constitution. A better answer is that we are political animals. None of us is the beast or god, in Aristotle's phrase, who can claim the strength of having lived outside the city and consented to enter its gates. We are born in political communities and exist in political communities. From this we incur obligations to those in the past who built and defended these institutions and those in the future who entrust us to pass them on, perhaps improved but nonetheless intact.

The idea that deliberate majorities obligated to their past are responsible for constitutionalism, it must be emphasized, is entirely compatible with individual liberty. The question is not whether the individual is protected, but rather who protects him or her, and how. Advocates of judicial engagement, skipping a step in the argument, have merely assumed the answer is judges. It is consequently vital to state this axiom before proceeding: *That an issue is constitutional does not necessarily make it judicial.* At the Constitutional Convention, James Madison doubted whether the Supreme Court should have jurisdiction in "all" constitutional cases, preferring instead that its authority be limited to cases "of a judiciary nature," meaning those that naturally came within the judicial ambit. But the Court would not have limitless authority to resolve all constitutional disputes. The delegates deemed Madison's amendment unnecessary because its premise was so obvious. John Marshall, who did not generally shrink from assertions of judicial power, echoed this sentiment in *Cohens v. Virginia*: the Constitution "does not extend the judicial power to every violation of the Constitution which may possibly take place, but to a 'case in law or equity,' in which a right, under such law, is asserted in a Court of justice. If the question cannot be brought into a Court, then there is no case in law or equity, and no jurisdiction is given by the words of [Article III]."[56]

Roger Pilon, a leader in the judicial engagement movement, attributes the opposite position to Madison, quoting him as calling an independent judiciary "the bulwark of our liberties." I am unable to locate this locution in Madison's writings on any topic, and as will be seen in chapter 3, there is much that militates against it. Nonetheless, in a highly influential 1991 essay in the *Wall Street Journal,* Pilon called on conservatives to reject the "majoritarianism that grew out of the Progressive

Era" in favor of what he presented as the Founders' position that judges would protect individual rights "especially from the majority." But if majoritarianism was a Progressive position, that movement must have drawn it in turn from Madison himself, whose tenth *Federalist* merely assumes "the republican principle" of majority rule and sets forth his method of working within it. Pilon, by contrast, issued a blanket declaration that the Founding vision "begins with individual liberty. It secures that liberty by constituting a government of separated and divided powers. And it subjects those powers to the principled scrutiny of an independent judiciary." Yet the judiciary is one of these powers, subject itself to the competing tensions between them. *Federalist* no. 51, the essay that elucidates the American system of separation of powers, nowhere describes judges as supervisors of that mechanism.[57]

In reality, *The Federalist* assumes both that the sole protection—the only effective protection—for rights comes from seasoned, deliberate majorities themselves; and, crucially, that there is no particular reason to believe judges would be any better at this protection than the people. Even within the confines of *Federalist* no. 78, Publius's most explicit defense of judicial review, that authority largely appears as a defense of the people against the regime, not of minorities against majorities. Judicial review, as has been seen, should be used to defend rather than impede deliberate majority rule reflected in the constitutive will of the people. The Framers were classically educated men who recognized the nobility in the political. And that, ultimately, is what we stand to lose if judicial engagement succeeds in elevating the individual over the city.

2. The Politics of Obligation

[T]he science of jurisprudence, the pride of the human intellect, which, with all its defects, redundancies, and errors, is the collected reason of ages, combining the principles of original justice with the infinite variety of human concerns.

—Edmund Burke[1]

Amid his infatuation with the French Revolution, America's minister to that country, Thomas Jefferson, dispatched a letter to his friend James Madison that reflected the enthusiasms to which the former was prone. He announced that he had used demographic data to tabulate the average length of a generation at nineteen years and wrote that society could not justly contract debts beyond that period. He meant to be taken literally. The reason was that the dead had no right to bind the living. Jefferson argued *"that the earth belongs in usufruct to the living,"* such that generations past could exercise no power nor claim any right over it.[2] The practical barriers to Jefferson's suggestion are insurmountable, beginning with the fact that generations drift in and out on a river of time rather than springing spontaneously into existence and then departing the scene. More important, it takes little reflection to see that no human endeavor could endure within these confines, and not just because, as Burke notes, humanity's noblest ends take several generations.

Madison sensed this. In a masterful refutation of Jefferson that adapts Locke while anticipating Burke, Madison observed that the earth belonged to the living only in its "natural state." By contrast, "[t]he *improvements* made by the dead form a charge against the living who take the benefit of them. This charge can no otherwise be satisfyed [*sic*] than by executing the will of the dead accompanying the improvements."[3]

This response must, or at least should, alarm proponents of judicial engagement, for it is profoundly antipresentist. On the contrary, far from anchoring politics in contemporary tastes alone, it says we have obligations not just to one another but also to the dead. Madison's response reflects what I shall call "the politics of obligation," and it anchors republican constitutionalism. The term is usually used to refer to the puzzle of obligation—why individuals should feel obligated to a regime—but I use it here, as I shall explain, to refer to the privilege of obligation. Both terms—politics and obligation—are important. Aristotle wrote that the political life was best for man. Tocqueville seconded this by seeing political activity as one antidote to the pathology of individualism. This is the sense in which politics is good for us. But it is not enough to explain fealty to the Constitution as originally understood. For that, we need obligation. We are obligated to this Constitution because it is ours, because our ancestors formulated it and our descendants will inherit it.

That is not to say the obligation is limitless. The Declaration of Independence speaks of our right to revolt against an oppressive government, but it also clearly confines that to the most extraordinary circumstances ("a long train of abuses"). Most important, revolt is an *extra*constitutional act, not one the Constitution itself licenses. It is, in Locke's terms, an "appeal to Heaven." Reform achieved within the constitutional system should aim, on the grounds of obligation elucidated below, to seek to restore, as Burke would say, its original principles, not to replace them.

REPUBLICANISM VS. LIBERTARIANISM

Republicanism seeks to recover the classical goods of politics—activity, interpersonal connection, and obligation—but without the pathologies, such as faction, that result from its forms. It is rooted, as we have seen, in the Latin from which it takes its name: the res publica, the public thing, occupying a space between the people and the state where political activity occurs. Republicanism encourages public deliberation about important and often unselfish matters while reflecting the deliberate and settled values of the community by means of representation. It thus encourages political activity but allows it to bind ultimately, not immediately.

It is opposed, fundamentally, to libertarian individualism, which sees the res publica in individualist terms. It is no coincidence that the vast bulk of adherents of judicial engagement are libertarians, for the theory, again, is fundamentally concerned with impeding government action. Jesse Merriam, a student of the conservative legal movement, has noted that given the left-leaning politics of law faculties, and the fact that most of those who lean right are libertarians, judicial engagement will inevitably take a turn in that direction. That is true, but it is equally true that libertarianism is philosophically endemic to judicial engagement.[4] Its central object is the inhibition of politics, which is one reason why, as chapter 3 will address, the legal turn—the move toward seeing the Constitution as a legal document written in legal language—is not only libertarian but also antipolitical.

It is true, as Eugene W. Hickok and Gary L. McDowell write, that the judiciary's rise is attributable in part to Congress's abdication, but that does not justify abandoning republican government. They wrote in 1993: "A once healthy regard for democratic decision-making and representation has run up against a distrust of democracy coupled with a hopeful embrace of judicial power to provide just resolutions to society's most pressing problems."[5] By contrast, judicial engagement has flat out given up on republicanism. Clark M. Neily III, for example, writes:

> With trillions of dollars in play every year and constituents who expect a steady supply of pork from Washington, there is no realistic prospect of the system reforming itself from the inside. Nor is it a matter of "throwing the bums out." The vast majority of public officials are decent, patriotic people who take seriously their duty to act in the public good. But the incentives to exercise forbidden powers and cater to interest groups are simply too strong.[6]

Timothy Sandefur similarly mocks a "throw the bums out" solution, observing that incumbents are entrenched and the tentacles of the administrative state are long, such that individual citizens cannot hope to overcome the barriers to registering their views or asserting their rights politically.[7]

In other words, voting, the most elemental civic activity, is unavailing. The assertiveness of citizens has failed and will continue to do so. One wonders whether, given their individualist and antimajoritarian sentiments, proponents of judicial engagement rue this at all. As for citizens, in our immovable passivity we do not even get the catharsis of thinking of the "government," that alien presence, as ridden with bums. Instead, these are decent people who cannot control their political appetites, which makes one wonder what makes them—or the constituents who "expect a steady supply of pork"—so decent. Neily as much as says that politics is hopeless and that our only path forward is judicial guardianship. Why judges do not have the same incentive to aggrandize their powers is unclear: again, the Paradox of Engagement. The basic job of these judges is to say "no," but what the courts often disallow majorities from doing is a fundamentally republican act: expressing their values on the basis of deliberation and representation. The individual's "freedom from" often conflicts with the community's "freedom to," with the latter referring not merely to plundering the oppressed but often simply to expressing its values or creating environments hospitable to them. They may, for example, want to say public prayers or limit pornographic displays, both of which the Supreme Court has made more challenging.

These are, in short, incompatible approaches to political life. One cares about what is "mine," the other about what human beings living in particular communities share. One sees the individual as isolated, the other as politically situated. One, courtesy of John Stuart Mill, would impose the same standard on all politics everywhere, while the other would embrace the variety of political life. One sees self-restraint, civility, and compromise as political virtues, the other as political impositions. Both are concerned with the protection of individuals on the basis of mutual and historical commitments, but one, libertarianism, would outsource that protection to a purportedly neutral, apolitical institution—the judiciary, whose members we are supposed simply to trust, even though we cannot trust anyone else—while the other, republicanism, including among republican virtues the majority's ability to see a public good beyond itself that embraces the protection of individuals, understands that all rights have limits and the political process itself, acting deliberately, must find them. One is based on isolation, the other on the interpersonal.

ARISTOTLE'S NOBLE POLITICS

The nobility of politics rings hollow if not altogether dissonant in contemporary ears because the word "politics" has been corrupted as a synonym for "government" and because government, in turn, is regarded with cheap cynicism that, at least institutionally, it sometimes merits and often does not. If we understand politics classically, in terms of shared endeavor directed toward the common good, we begin to recover its noble character. Politics is, in this sense, inherently interpersonal, for it pertains to things that are common. But Aristotle understood that it was intrinsically public in another sense: people could not pursue the just or practice the virtues alone.

Aristotle's dictum that "man is a political animal" is well known, but its use as an aphorism strips it of the richness of its context. Aristotle arrives at this conclusion by asking what makes human beings, among other creatures, unique. The answer is that "man alone among the animals has speech." Other animals, too, can communicate, but only pain and pleasure, whereas "it is peculiar to man as compared to the other animals that he alone has a perception of good and bad and just and unjust and the other things of this sort; and community in these things is what makes a household and a city." Politics is thus directed inherently toward higher ends and is, since it is rooted in speech, intrinsically an interpersonal activity. The isolated person on a desert island cannot pursue the good and the bad and the just and the unjust because he or she cannot articulate those concepts to others who listen, respond, and act upon them.

This is different in a crucial way from the Platonic concept of the

Forms. In the Allegory of the Cave in Plato's *Republic,* the rare and true philosopher emerges from the obscuring shadows of the cave to contemplate the pure forms—something like objective truths, including the form of justice—in the heavens in what appears to be a solitary and receptive pursuit. This account is layered in irony, and we must take care not to oversimplify Plato's teaching, for it emerges not from either solitude or passivity but rather from an active dialogue between Socrates and his interlocutors. Nevertheless, Aristotle's pursuit of justice is strikingly more interpersonal and active than the one Socrates elucidates in this part of the *Republic,* and it requires situation in a political context.

That does not mean Aristotle was a democrat, but he did recognize that majority rule might offer particular advantages. One came to be known as the wisdom of crowds. Aristotle surmised:

> The many, of whom none is individually an excellent man, nevertheless can when joined together be better—not as individuals but all together—than those [who are best], just as dinners contributed by many can be better than those equipped from a single expenditure. For because they are many, each can have a part of virtue and prudence, and on their joining together, the multitude, with its many feet and hands and having many senses, becomes like a single human being, and so also with respect to character and mind.[8]

The many each have a part of "virtue and prudence," which is to say they are not best in the aggregate at deciding merely on tax or health care policy—though these do touch on questions of justice and are subsumed under his discussion of the "advantageous"—but also with respect to questions of the noble and good. This is, for Aristotle, what politics means—not the trappings or institutions of government per se but rather the common pursuit of advantageous and just ends. People who are engaged in such pursuits are engaged in politics, rightly understood. It was much later that the idea of a radical division between the public and private spheres emerged as a defining feature of modern liberal politics. But even this feature, which assigns certain goods to the political realm and reserves others to the private, retains an ample space both for politics and, crucially, for the inherently political authority to decide which goods belong in which realm.

Aristotle believed, furthermore, in something libertarian theorists deny: the existence of community. In his *Politics,* he defines good and bad regimes according to which serve the interests of the ruled and which exist for the sake of the ruler. Democracy is a bad regime: the many ruling for their own sake. But this is something of a puzzle. A good regime rules for the sake of the ruled, and the many—who compose, after all, the vast bulk of the community—are ruling for themselves. Why is democracy not inherently, even by definition, a good regime? Aristotle insists that it is not, calling our attention instead to the politeia, or polity, as the healthy version of rule by the community. The reason is that the "ruled" do not consist of the many as isolated, detached individuals. They form a political community with ontological status and a good that cannot be merely equated with the good of all the individuals, a distinction similar to Rousseau's between the general will and the will of all. Otherwise, he writes, "the community becomes an alliance, which differs from others—from alliances of remote allies—only by location, and law becomes a compact and, as the sophist Lycophron said, a guarantor among one another of the just things, but not the sort of thing to make the citizens good and just." In the very roots of Aristotle's political reflection, society rises from a series of expanding partnerships that begin with the family and end with the city. The individual of the libertarian ethos is nowhere to be found.

THE INDIVIDUALIST TURN

Many libertarians instead turn to the purported individualism of John Locke, whom advocates of judicial engagement often invoke to support an individualist and presentist constitution. Yet Locke wove an elaborate tale of the state of nature only to conclude, with apparent simplicity, that governments were flatly majoritarian. "When any number of Men have so consented to make one Community or Government, they are thereby presently incorporated, and make one Body Politick, wherein the Majority have a Right to act and conclude the rest."⁹ Locke supplied several reasons for this, including the necessity for the political body to act and the impossibility of doing so unanimously—another reminder that action, not just inhibition of it, is a political function. Another reason for Locke's majoritarianism, importantly, was that unless one had to obey the majority, one would be under no more obligations than one had faced in the state of nature, so the contract by which one had entered society would have been for naught. For in the absence of acknowledging the majority's authority, individuals would simply judge for themselves. Locke wondered: "What new Engagement if he were no farther tied by any Decrees of the Society, than he himself thought fit, and did actually consent to? This would be Still as great a liberty, as he himself had before his Compact, or any one else in the State of Nature hath, who may submit himself and consent to any acts of it if he thinks fit."

Locke was not an absolute majoritarian. He told the state-of-nature story exactly because he believed the political community was legitimately entitled to rule only with respect to public ends. What he recognized was that the authority to decide what these are is itself an immense power. Locke is sometimes invoked in assigning that power to the judiciary, and if we read him superficially, and contemporarily, he can seem to lend support to that judgment. He does, after all, define the state of nature as a condition in which "there is no Judge to be found" and in which people consequently settle differences by appealing to force. Randy Barnett and Evan Bernick, for example, use Locke's reference to the lack of a "known and indifferent judge" in the state of nature to help elucidate the purpose of Article III judges under the Constitution.¹⁰ Yet in using the term "Judge," Locke refers not to an Article III–type court but rather to the supreme authority of the regime, which is the legislative. He thus writes that the creation of political society "set[s] up a Judge on Earth. . . . Which Judge is the Legislative, or Magistrates appointed by it."¹¹ The purpose the state-of-nature story serves for Locke is much like Madison's for the Bill of Rights, as we shall see in chapter 4. Its purpose is to provide a common understanding of rights and the proper scope of the community's authority, not to remove such questions from the community's hands altogether.

The genuine sources of the individualist Constitution lie not in Aristotle or Locke but rather in Hobbes and Rousseau.[12] Locke's state of nature was relatively peaceable and social. Hobbes's, by contrast, consisted solely of rapacious, isolated individuals. Hobbes's literary nemesis Aristotle, who said the tyrant seeks to prevent independent associations and thought, would have understood the inexorable ascent, or perhaps descent, Hobbes makes from the isolated and therefore insecure individual to a flattened and tyrannical social structure that consists only of those individuals and the Leviathan that rules them. Rousseau started from similarly individualist conceptions but with a different view of natural man: his "noble savage" was asocial, carefree, and happy until corrupted by society and enslaved by politics. Yet strikingly, proceeding from this individual outward, Rousseau arrives at exactly the same kind of totalizing politics as Hobbes. The difference is that what Hobbes calls the Leviathan is for Rousseau the general will from which no rational person would, and no citizen is allowed to, dissent.

Neither of these is a classically American view, which, again, mediates between the classical and modern. As Jefferson's letter about the provenance of the Declaration of Independence indicates, the Founders' understanding of politics owed more to the classical Greeks and the majoritarian Locke than to any individualist tradition. Justice Bushrod Washington, President Washington's nephew and the inheritor of his estate at Mount Vernon, occupies a particular place in the pantheon of judicial engagement as the most eloquent articulator of the "privileges and immunities" of American citizenship. Riding circuit in *Corfield v. Coryell,* Justice Washington felt these privileges and immunities were so obvious as to make their specification "tedious," though it is significant that he announces his intent to "confin[e]" them. "They may, however, be all comprehended under the following general heads: Protection by the government; the enjoyment of life and liberty, with the right to acquire and possess property of every kind, and to pursue and obtain happiness and safety; subject nevertheless to such restraints as the government may justly prescribe for the general good of the whole."

It is this last phrase—the subjection of rights to "the general good of the whole"—that proponents of judicial engagement, who apply this definition of privileges and immunities to the states through the Fourteenth Amendment, often overlook. This is key, among other reasons, because the content of the general good is not within the purview of judges. It is a matter of prudence and choice, not the application of law to cases. The only qualifier Justice Washington provides is that these restrictions must be "justly prescribed." This is different from saying the restrictions themselves must meet a substantive standard of justice. Rather, the point is that they must be prescribed by law accessible to all in advance.

TOCQUEVILLE'S POLITICS OF CONNECTION

Tocqueville wrote of another promise of a noble politics: it bridges the chasms that naturally separate democratic men. The French commentator was concerned with "individualism," which he called "a recent expression arising from a new idea. Our fathers knew only selfishness." Selfishness, a vice, was a narcissistic tendency to interpret everything in terms of oneself. Individualism was "a reflective and peaceable sentiment that disposes each citizen to isolate himself from the mass of those like him and to withdraw to one side with his family and his friends, so that after having thus created a little society for his own use, he willingly abandons society at large to itself." Individualism was a pathology of democracy, a political system under which individuals felt simultaneously all-powerful, leading them to spurn social and political connection, and weak, inducing them to defer to majority opinion. One result was that democracy was prone to mediocrity. For Tocqueville, the richness in life lay not in the isolated individual, who was debilitated in his or her loneliness, but rather in the connections between people: "Sentiments and ideas renew themselves, the heart is enlarged, and the human mind is developed only by the reciprocal action of men upon one another."

This reciprocal action was classically political in nature. Self-government, which was most potent at the local level, drew people out of their isolation into association with one another and, crucially for Tocqueville, spurred them to be active rather than inert. Fascinated by the phenomenon of local politics in America, he wrote:

> The legislators of America did not believe that, to cure a malady so natural to the social body in democratic times and so fatal, it was enough to accord to the nation as a whole a representation of itself; they thought that, in addition, it was fitting to give political life to each portion of the territory in order to multiply infinitely the occasions for citizens to act together and to make them feel every day that they depend on one another.

BURKE'S GENERATIONAL POLITICS

This is classical politics. To understand the particular politics of *obligation*, we must turn to Burke. Burke understood tradition to be the storehouse of wisdom accumulated over time, the theater in which the fixed principles of objective morality and truth play out in the infinitely variable scenes of human circumstance. No one man possessed sufficient wisdom to decide questions of justice divorced from the concreteness of circumstances, and tradition is the accumulation of both. He thus said his British forebears displayed "[a] politic caution, a guarded circumspection, a moral rather than a complexional timidity." This last phrase—moral rather than complexional timidity—is one of the most beautiful and revealing in the Burkean corpus. It reminds us, especially against an Enlightenment-obsessed jurisprudence that seeks always to know what is "rational," that human beings are flawed and that humility about that fact is a virtue. Consequently, Burke said British statesmen "acted under a strong impression of the ignorance and fallibility of mankind."[13]

Hence his suspicion of a politics of natural rights. They existed, he wrote, but were not the reason for government because they were ill-suited to the complexities of postlapsarian man. "[T]heir abstract perfection is their practical defect," he wrote. "By having a right to every thing they want every thing. Government is a contrivance of human wisdom to provide for human *wants*."[14] Instead of universalistic natural rights, Burke regarded rights as "entailed inheritances,"[15] not because he did not believe some rights were universal, but rather because he believed their concrete expression in bounded political communities was the best, indeed the only, guarantor of their attainment and protection. This is as opposed to rights as pure and ungrounded philosophical abstractions, which suffered from the dual defect of being impossible to instantiate and, because it was too tempting to rid society of "irrational" impediments to progress, prone to abuse.

Peter J. Stanlis has shown that Burke did believe vigorously in natural law.[16] That much is evident in Burke's years-long, some say obsessive, impeachment of Warren Hastings, the governor-general of the British East India Company. Hastings was accused of presiding over the rape and plunder of India, and in his famous speech to the lords presenting the indictment, Burke declared that he impeached Hastings "in the name of human nature itself." But he equally impeached him "in the name of the Commons of Great Britain in Parliament assembled"; that is, in the name of a particular political community.

The fullness of the politics of obligation arises through Burke's challenge to the social-contract theorizing that was popular at the time, and which formed an unquestionable rhetorical trope—though not, arguably, as much of a substantive method—in the early American republic. Burke wrote:

> Society is indeed a contract. Subordinate contracts, for objects of mere occasional interest, may be dissolved at pleasure; but the state ought not to be considered as nothing better than a partnership agreement in a trade of pepper and coffee, callico or tobacco, or some other such low concern, to be taken up for a little temporary

interest, and to be dissolved by the fancy of the parties. It is to be looked on with other reverence; because it is not a partnership in things subservient only to the gross animal existence of a temporary and perishable nature. It is a partnership in all science; a partnership in all art; a partnership in every virtue, and in all perfection. As the ends of such a partnership cannot be obtained in many generations, it becomes a partnership not only between those who are living, but between those who are living, those who are dead, and those who are to be born.[17]

Burke recognizes both the nobility of politics and the crucial fact governing the boundaries of the social contract, which is that its ends and thus its obligations are transgenerational. Those who advocate a presentist constitutionalism would profit from his admonition:

But one of the first and most leading principles on which the commonwealth and the laws are consecrated, is lest the temporary possessors and life-renters in it, unmindful of what they have received from their ancestors, or of what is due to their posterity, should act as if they were the entire masters; that they should not think it amongst their rights to cut off the entail, or commit waste on the inheritance, by destroying at their pleasure the whole original fabric of their society; hazarding to leave to those who come after them, a ruin instead of an habitation, and teaching these successors as little to respect their contrivances, as they had themselves respected the institutions of their forefathers. By this unprincipled facility of changing the state as often, and as much, and in as many ways, as there are floating fancies or fashions, the whole chain and continuity of the commonwealth would be broken. No one generation could link with the other. Men would become little better than the flies of a summer.[18]

This idea of the regime as an inheritance provides, in Burke's words, "a sure principle of conservation, and a sure principle of transmission;

without at all excluding a principle of improvement."[19] The politics of obligation leaves room for reform, but, as Burke writes, it is reform for the sake of restoring original values. In the same way that it is wrong to demolish for contemporary interest or taste a home that has been passed through many generations because doing so violates obligations to both one's ancestors and one's descendants, altering the regime casually breaks a promise we make when taking our place as citizens. Advocates of judicial engagement of course seek to preserve that promise, but only because it is advantageous, not because generational promises bind us ethically. As we have seen, their theories expose the Constitution to constant scrutiny and change based on the judgments of the here and now.

This bears careful attention, especially since, again, most advocates of originalism seek to preserve a political inheritance. The problem is that there is no inherent reason, on their account, why we should. We have no duty to do so, only our contemporary judgment that hewing to the Philadelphia Constitution is advantageous. As Keith Whittington has noted, originalism is an interpretive method. It cannot account for the justice of the instrument being interpreted. The politics of obligation can, but the individualist Constitution rejects it: we abide by the Constitution and interpret it faithfully because, on some accounts, it is good for us now; because, on others, we consent to it now; or because, on other readings still, it protects our liberties now. But the standard is always "now."

PRESENTISM AND CONSTITUTIONALISM: A SAMPLING OF VIEWS

This is far more vulnerable to living constitutionalism than the proponents of judicial engagement admit. Neither they nor living constitutionalists can ground their views in a theory of obligation; many of the New Originalists simply believe they have a better interpretive framework for understanding the Constitution. There is no home in judicial engagement for the Burkean notion of wisdom accumulating across generations or of obligation accruing to one's ancestors and descendants alike, a view we have seen that James Madison shared. Republican constitutionalism hinges on it.

Views among originalists as to what creates a duty to obey are varied. Barnett argues that "popular sovereignty" resides in "the people as individuals." On this account, a constitution's purpose is not, despite what Madison said, to actuate a majority's deliberate choices. There is no such thing as the political community *as* community governing. Instead, individuals delegate the power to govern to "a small subset" of the people whose legitimate purposes are limited to the objects and rules according to which authority was constituted. As we have already seen, Barnett contrasts this "Republican Constitution," in which rights antedate government, to a "Democratic Constitution" that defines and grants liberties. Chapter 4 will discuss this distinction in more detail, but what is important for the question of obligation is that a Republican Constitution commands it only because our contemporary individual rights are paramount. Note the temporal standard: "Ultimately what matters, however, is not the labels we use to describe these differing views of popular sovereignty, or what they were called in the past. Nor does it really matter which exact view was held by those who wrote the Constitution. What matters is the type of constitution they wrote and whether we *today* believe it to be a good enough constitution to follow."[20] Obligation is in its essence a question of the present.

Hadley Arkes, the preeminent theorist of natural law constitutionalism, contrasts it with tradition. The invocation of custom "is a movement . . . from an independent ground of right and wrong—from a moral understanding that does not depend on the vagaries of local cultures—to a ground of jurisprudence that reduces to the 'habits of the tribe,' or to the opinions that are dominant in a particular country." Arkes goes so far as to associate this kind of jurisprudence with "cultural relativism" and "the legal arguments cast up by Roger Taney and Stephen Douglas, in their defense of American slavery. In our own time . . . [t]here will be an appeal, at a critical point, to 'shared understandings' or 'political traditions,' in place of moral truths, as the ultimate ground of our jurisprudence."[21] These are strange authorities for Arkes to criticize since both regarded the Supreme Court as the ultimate disposer of constitutional questions. In his famed 1987 address "On the Authoritativeness of Supreme Court Decisions," Attorney General Edwin S. Meese, arguing the distinction between the Constitution and constitutional law, noted Douglas's claim that "[i]t is the fundamental principle of the judiciary that its decisions are final. It is created for that purpose so that when you cannot agree among yourselves on a disputed point you appeal to the judicial tribunal which steps in and decides for you, and that decision is binding on every good citizen."[22]

Moreover, Taney and Douglas are strange company in which to place a thinker like St. Thomas Aquinas, who equated custom with Aristotelian habituation toward virtue. Following Aristotle, Aquinas explains that "a change in the law considered simply as such is detrimental to the common well-being, because custom has great force in securing the observance of laws, inasmuch as what is done contrary to custom, even in trivial matters, is regarded as grave."[23] For Aquinas as, later, for Burke, custom is encoded in the traditions of the common law, whose principles "are called the *nurseries of virtue.*"[24] Madison, too, is cast from the pantheon by this reasoning, since his *Federalist* no. 49 says a regime will find it useful "to have the prejudices of the community on its side."[25]

For his part, Burke's position was hardly that there were no moral truths; it was that they were likeliest to be discovered and, crucially, maintained through the accretion of tradition than through constant reanalysis using the tools of contemporary reason. Reason errs, and it does not always command the same loyalty as traditions knitted into a political culture's genetic code. Tradition, of course, can be monstrously applied, but so can our rational faculties. The Progressivism that produced *Buck v. Bell* was much more associated with the intoxication of scientism than with tradition. Both are subject to boundaries, but Burke was not a cultural relativist. Since his insights, it has typically been a conservative belief that those exulting in the reveries of reason are more prone to engage in abuse than those anchored in custom and tradition.

That judges would not always reach what Arkes regards as the right conclusions is evident in his extensive differences with a libertarian constitutionalist who would employ the same methods. Sandefur argues that the Declaration of Independence is "a legal document" that "anchors our legal and political system on a firm philosophical ground."[26] The declaration, on Sandefur's account, provides an interpretive framework for the Constitution. The reason is the primacy it places on rights: "People are born with liberty; their rights are not privileges that government gives to them as it pleases. Legitimate government is based on, and bound by, their rights, and nobody—no king, no legislature, no democratic majority—has any basic entitlement to control them. Freedom is the starting point of politics; government's powers are secondary and derivative, and therefore limited."[27] Two things merit notice: The first is that the Constitution rests on "philosophical" ground. This implies presentism: our obligation to the Constitution rests on the persuasiveness of its philosophy, not on any sense of patriotic duty, in the here and now.[28] Second, Sandefur, perhaps most explicitly among advocates of judicial engagement, understands politics in terms of the isolated individual. As the starting point of politics, "freedom" means each individual's freedom from the others. There is no place here for either a politics of obligation or Arkes's moral conservatism.

John O. McGinnis and Michael B. Rappaport argue that the Constitution deserves loyalty because it is a good one, and its goodness can only be realized if we follow the intent of its enactors. But their underlying standard, again, is presentist: we are not bound to the Constitution by generational ties of obligation but rather by our contemporary judgment that it is good for us: "Law in general, and constitutional law in particular, should be measured by its contribution to our current welfare." As they also put it, "Our normative approach to constitutions and interpretation is welfare consequentialist. We believe that constitutions and interpretive methods should be assessed based on their consequences for the welfare of the people of the nation."[29] This is of course true as far as it goes. Burke's argument is not that happiness does not matter but rather that the accumulated wisdom of custom is likelier to conduce to it than contemporary philosophical investigation.

But obligation also matters. On the McGinnis-Rappaport argument, it is fair to subject the Constitution to relentless inspection—which they have undertaken and found the document to be good by virtue of its supermajority requirements—but the simple notion that we might be obliged to the work of our ancestors and the inheritance of our descendants finds no place. We are obliged to the Constitution only because it is good for us today; there is no generational character to the argument, nor is there genuine obligation beneath it—unless obligation means obligation to one's own immediate and individual good, which certainly requires no virtue and may on the contrary be an expression of patent selfishness.

Whittington has steered a middle and more persuasive course, writing of "potential sovereignty" that the people can take up when they please but whose most recent results are binding until they do. "[T]he people do not and cannot be understood to renew constantly their consent to the government and its constitutional form. Rather, the people emerge at particular historical moments to deliberate on constitutional issues and to provide binding expressions of their will, which are to serve as fundamental law in the future when the sovereign is absent."[30] Yet this approach, too, is laced with presentism—even in its latent form, sovereignty is always exercised at discrete moments, never generationally—and this account fails to explain why we should not prescribe Jefferson's frequent constitutional renewals so that potential sovereignty *can* be actualized. One of Whittington's objections to tacit consent is that the consent is never actually exercised. Yet this is an easy problem to fix—that is, by scheduling regular opportunities for actualizing sovereignty—and one wonders why Whittington does not.

LIBERALISM AND JUDICIAL RESTRAINT

Before turning to the question of judicial engagement more generally, it may be worth noting that conservatives are hardly the only stripe of judges to have found themselves in possession of judicial power after critiquing its excessive use. Many of the New Deal justices, such as William O. Douglas, preached restraint on economic rights but proceeded to become absolutists on what are known as "personal" rights under the Warren Court. The false distinction between "economic" and "personal" rights is indicative of the problem. There were, however, both judges and legal scholars who wrestled with these issues more consistently, and we can profitably learn from them.

Judge Learned Hand, generally regarded as the greatest American jurist not to sit on the Supreme Court, ran for office in New York on the Progressive ticket. As a judge, he was a model of principled restraint in a career that spanned the era of economic reform to the explosion of personal rights. In his clearest statement of his judicial philosophy, the Oliver Wendell Holmes Lectures published as 1958's *The Bill of Rights*, Hand argued that judicial review is not implicit in the Constitution, but it is necessary to the governing framework's successful operation. The contingent nature of this authority was a reason to confine its use: judicial review "need not be exercised whenever a court sees, or thinks that it sees, an invasion of the Constitution. It is always a preliminary question how importunately the occasion demands an answer."[31] Consequently, "it was absolutely essential to confine the power [of judicial review] to the need that evoked it: that is, it was and always has been necessary to distinguish between the frontiers of another 'Department's' authority and the propriety of its choices within those frontiers."[32] Judge William H. Pryor Jr. has shown that this narrative of *Marbury v. Madison* inventing judicial review, which was actually long established, emerged as a Progressive trope in reaction to judges disallowing economic reforms.[33] Hand has the distinction of applying the resultant doctrine of restraint consistently even when progressives obtained judicial power and found it available for pursuing their preferred ends. Hand warned that the judge declaring the manner in which Congress may address a perceived problem was inescapably in a similar position to the legislator balancing values: "True, courts might, and indeed they always do, disclaim authority to intervene. Unless they are sure beyond doubt that the compromise imposed is wrong; but that does not disguise the fact that their choice is an authentic exercise of the same process that produced the statute itself."[34]

The courts had shown this in the inconsistency of their economic decisions, especially in their attempts to ascertain legislative motives, but "the answer becomes decidedly more obscure when the statute touches those other interests, now called 'Personal Rights.'"[35] In the cases of these interests, Hand found it untenable to claim that the Bill of Rights, and especially the Fifth Amendment, "constituted severer restrictions as to Liberty than Property." A judge was no more qualified to replace the legislature's balancing of interests in the case of personal than of economic rights.[36] The proper judicial inquiry was whether a wrong was within Congress's power to address, not whether legislators addressed it compatibly with a judge's preferences. The latter assertion of authority would make the Court "a third legislative chamber," and if one was needed, "it should appear for what it is, and not as the interpreter of inscrutable principles."[37]

Like Hand, Justice Felix Frankfurter displayed an admirable consistency between his New Deal judicial deference and his comparable restraint when "personal rights" became the focus of the Warren Court. Before joining the Court, as it was still invalidating pillars of the New Deal, Frankfurter emphasized the limitation of judicial authority to cases and controversies. "The Court is not the forum for a chivalrous or disinterested defense of the Constitution. Its business is with self-regarding, immediate, secular claims. Legislation will not be struck down except to vindicate a legally protected interest; damage alone is not enough."[38] The requirements of standing confined the scope of constitutional dispute, as did "[t]he Court's general doctrine of avoidance of constitutional adjudication. . . . Needless clash with the legislature is avoided by construing statutes so as to save them, if it can be done without doing violence to the habits of English speech." Frankfurter warned on the grounds "of the highest judicial statesmanship" against deciding cases more broadly than necessary because doing so "foreclos[ed] the future." Significantly, he credited Justice John Marshall's opinion in *Fletcher v. Peck* with the "magistral formulation" of judicial review: that is, he credited judicial review of a state statute in *Fletcher* rather than with review of a congressional enactment in *Marbury.*" For Frankfurter, James Bradley Thayer gave judicial review "its most luminous exposition."[39]

In 1955, Frankfurter, who had been serving on the Court since 1939, gave an address at Harvard Law School that was published as "John Marshall and the Judicial Function."[40] The date is significant. Earl Warren had become chief justice in 1953 and had ordered a reargument of *Brown v. Board of Education,* a case chapter 5 will treat more fully. On some reports, Frankfurter, a political liberal who had been affiliated with both the American Civil Liberties Union and the National Association for the Advancement of Colored People, was initially reluctant on grounds of judicial restraint to declare segregated schools unconstitutional, though he ultimately voted with a unanimous Court to do so.

In his 1955 remarks, Frankfurter narrowly construed the power of the Court on which he sat, arguing that Marshall would have done so as well. In Marshall's time, "[t]he Constitution was not thought of as the repository of the supreme law limiting all government, with a court wielding the deepest-cutting power of deciding whether there is any authority in government at all to do what is sought to be done."[41] Frankfurter feared "a vast enveloping present-day role of law" that arose from a century of economic change. Like Hand, though, he implied the Court's application of doctrines of restraint and assertiveness was inconsistent between economic and personal rights. "[N]o judge charged with the duty of enforcing the Due Process clauses of the Fifth and Fourteenth Amendments, and the Equal Protection of the Laws Clause of the Fourteenth Amendment, can free himself from the disquietude that the line is often very thin between the cases in which the Court felt compelled to abstain from adjudication because of their 'political' nature, and the cases that so frequently arise in applying the concepts of 'liberty' and 'equality.'"[42] He continued with a warning that liberal activism would license a new era of conservative activism on behalf of economic rights. "Yesterday the active area in this field was concerned with 'property.' Today it is 'civil liberties.' Tomorrow it may again be 'property.' Who can say that in a society with a mixed economy, like ours, these two areas are sharply separated, and that certain freedoms in relation to property may not again be deemed, as they were in the past, aspects of individual freedom?"[43] Law could not be reduced to "a technical doctrine of judicial authority."[44]

Significantly, Frankfurter described this as the view of government of "an old-fashioned liberal" who was committed "to the humane and gradualist tradition in dealing with refractory social and political problems, recognizing them to be fractious because of their complexity and not amenable to quick and propitious solutions without resort to methods which deny law as the instrument and offspring of reason."[45] Judges should know the limits of their positions: "If judges want to be preachers, they should dedicate themselves to the pulpit; if judges want to be primary shapers of policy, the legislature is their place. Self-willed judges are the least defensible offenders against government under law."[46]

Frankfurter declined to operate as such a judge even when positions he had long maintained in politics were at stake. He dissented in 1943's *West Virginia State Board of Education v. Barnette*,[47] famously arguing that despite being a member of a vilified minority as a Jew, he could not allow that perspective to intrude on his judicial views. He dissented from *Mapp v. Ohio's*[48] imposition of the exclusionary rule on the states as well as from *Baker v. Carr's* interference in the drawing of legislative districts. The point is not that he was always right in these matters. His initial doubt about *Brown*—though his record on desegregation was impeccable in other cases, including his masterful concurrence in *Cooper v. Aaron*—elevated an ethic of restraint over a clear constitutional prohibition. The same is true of *Barnette*. Restraint, as we shall see in considering cases in chapter 5, is not an unvarnished good. But unlike other justices such as Douglas or William Brennan, Frankfurter has the considerable distinction of consistency.

So did one of the dominant legal minds of the era, Alexander M. Bickel. Bickel, like Hand, saw judicial review as conjured, "summoned up out of the constitutional vapors, shaped, and maintained."[49] For Bickel, *Marbury* may have been an "accident" of history that endured because "Marshall's own view of the scope of legislative power had grandeur."[50] Because it exerted a "counter-majoritarian force" and its power of judicial review was "a deviant institution in the American democracy,"[51] the Court was bound to exercise "the passive virtues."

Bickel denied a judicial duty to decide all constitutional cases. Importantly, he introduced the idea of judicial prudence in avoiding the exercise of judicial review, especially with respect to political questions, which presented "something greatly more flexible, something of prudence, not construction and principle."[52] The Court could not reduce the question of which cases it would take to algorithms, but that did not mean it wielded "unchanneled, undirected, uncharted discretion . . . proceeding from impulse, hunch, sentiment, predilection, inarticulable and unreasoned. The antithesis of principle in an institution that represents decency and reason is not whim or even expediency, but prudence."[53]

One example of the exercise of that prudence was the Court's initial refusal, in *Poe v. Ullman*,[54] to overturn an unenforced Connecticut statute prohibiting birth control. For Bickel, the Court's refusal to acknowledge standing represented a prudential recognition of a political accommodation in the state according to which the laws would remain on the books but would not be enforced: "It may be that the exquisite balance registered by the disused yet unrepealed Connecticut statute is just what suits the people of Connecticut."[55] In any event, "[i]f Catholic opinion in Connecticut and officials who are responsive to it cannot decide whether it is wise or self-defeating to forbid the use of contraceptives by authority of the state, it is quite wrong for the Court to relieve them of this burden of self-government."[56]

Bickel's subtle treatment of the 1961 case of *Garner v. Louisiana* also illustrates the importance of judicial prudence.[57] The case concerned a sit-in protest at a segregated lunch counter whose participants were prosecuted for disturbing the peace. *Garner* was the first case clearly presenting the question of whether the Fourteenth Amendment prohibited discrimination in private rather than public facilities. The dilemma was that the passive virtues would have declined to force the issue in the first case presenting it, yet avoiding the controversy would have imposed hardship on the protestors, who had been sentenced to months in jail.

"A sound judicial instinct will generally favor deflecting the problem in one or more initial cases, for there is much to be gained from letting it simmer, so that a mounting number of incidents exemplifying it may have a cumulative effect on the judicial mind as well as on public and professional opinion." But given the hardship of the prison sentences, Bickel would have resolved the issue on the vagueness of the statute against disturbing the peace.

What Hand, Frankfurter, and Bickel shared was a commitment to the craft of politics in all its nobility and occasional ugliness. Their judicial philosophies simply recognize that there is no other enduring means of resolving social disputes, as well as that solutions arrived at politically have the cementing effect of consensus. They recognize, as well, the role of a judge in a republican system, which is not to right all wrongs but rather to apply the law.

MADISON AND THE POLITICS OF OBLIGATION

Madison provides a compelling reason for infrequent recurrence to constitutional questions: constitutionalism would be impossible if one did. In *Federalist* no. 49, a reply to Jefferson's proposal for frequent constitutional conventions, Madison rejected presentism as incompatible with constitutionalism. Constitutions had only as much authority as the people gave them, which is itself a republican value, and that respect came only from time. Frequent challenges to the Constitution would "deprive the government of that veneration which time bestows on every thing, and without which perhaps the wisest and freest governments would not possess the requisite stability." Whereas Whittington says these moments of activated sovereignty provide an opportunity to "deliberate" on the Constitution, Madison is doubtful, preferring that the Constitution have "the prejudices of the community on its side." These prejudices ferment over generations because men's reason is fortified by the knowledge that evidence for the Constitution is "*ancient* as well as *numerous.*" This would not matter in a nation of philosophers, in which "[a] reverence for the laws would be sufficiently inculcated by the voice of an enlightened reason." However, such a condition is a mirage, "as little to be expected, as the philosophical race of kings wished for by Plato." Madison instead feared that the "public passions" typically govern constitutional questions.[58] The presentist may believe Madison's Constitution merits veneration, but this is no more than a contingency. If there were a better Constitution available—and one senses judicial engagement would not be hampered by humility in its design—we could replace ours. It is up to us to decide, free of any obligation but our own sense of our rights today.

Madison's bridge between Locke, on whose account a right of property arises from improving the natural condition, and Burke, who measures such improvements and thus rights generationally, forms a politics of obligation. It supplies, in turn, a normative basis for originalism, one that escapes individualist constitutionalism's fleeting desires of the here and now. We do not have to judge that the Constitution is good for us today. The inherent tunnel vision of the moment may, in a given instance, lead us astray. Instead, a politics of obligation itself can ground originalism: we are morally and politically obligated to our shared past and our descendants' future. The Constitution forms a transgenerational promise that we inherited and, just as important, will pass on. Burke's notion of wisdom accumulated over time through the medium of experience—a medium in which theory mixes with circumstances—is both grounding and humbling. It anchors political experience against the fancies to which pure, unmoored rationality is prone and which Burke correctly saw going haywire in the French Revolution. It is modest in disposition insofar as it acknowledges that what seems irrational in our heritage may have more to say for it than our contemporary reason recognizes because it reflects the compiled wisdom of generations who, especially when taken together, may have known something we have not grasped and perhaps cannot in a single generational moment.

This is the same concept that militates against convening, say, a meeting of the smartest law and political science professors to write the best constitution for our time. That is a shiver in search of a spine, not least because the horizon of the here and now is too limited a perspective. The inevitable mistakes that would occur would be amplified by the overconfident homage contemporary society pays to instantaneous reason. It may seem, of course, that such is exactly what the Framers of the Constitution—fifty-five men whom Jefferson famously described as "an assembly of demigods"—did in Philadelphia. It was not. The Framers invented hardly anything. Nearly every innovation was either compelled by circumstance, such as federalism, or adapted—such as the notions of separation of powers or of representation by filtration—from long-standing colonial forms.[59]

Neither presidents nor new citizens swear to uphold the best constitution they can conjure; they swear to preserve, protect, and defend *this* Constitution, *our* Constitution, and it is hard to see why if not for the politics of obligation. One can repair an ancestral home—though Burke would "make the reparation as nearly as possible in the style of the building"[60]—or renovate it modestly. Over time, modern conveniences will be installed. One can add to it in a way that enhances rather than diminishes the value of the inheritance. But to say simply that one possesses a title to this home in the here and now and thus can, without obligation to the past or future, tear it down or sell it off for contemporary advantage breaks a promise that lies at the heart of the politics of obligation. Yet proponents of judicial engagement who would never consider frittering away their children's college funds in order to sate their own material desires would expose the Constitution to precisely that.

It surely sounds strange to say that committed originalists are actually wasting a constitutional inheritance. But in freeing individuals from obligation and empowering them to make all choices—even if they constrain the manner of those choices to the arduous process of constitutional amendment—they risk the regime because they place it on a fragile foundation: our ability to choose wisely in the here and now despite being corrupted by impulse, tempted by appetites, and limited in vision. Without a politics of obligation, we are left constitutionally adrift. We lack what Madison in *Federalist* no. 49 called "prejudices" in favor of it. "Prejudice" may sound irrational. Who, after all, judges something before seeing it? But prejudice in the sense Madison meant it refers to the limits of our instantaneous reason, something our reason can itself recognize.

The normative basis of republican constitutionalism, then, is this: We owe a political debt to our forebears and descendants, and political activity fulfills our natures. An overactive judiciary severs the link between these values by supplanting the need for political activity. Rather than, for example, convincing our neighbors of our views or electing candidates who share them—activities that are classically political insofar as they involve a shared conception of the common good and the requirement to elevate that good over individual appetites—we stand in isolation before the bench, demanding that judges protect us.

Importantly, because nearly all our actions affect others, we are asking judges to impose our views of the good on others. Libertarian theory sees coercion as an inherent evil, to be avoided except at the cost of harming someone else. Conservatism sees political activity, nobly understood, as an inherent good that can promote higher ends than the loneliness of the judicially protected individual standing against the judicially restricted state. Popular sovereignty is not a self-justifying end; it serves the ends of political activity and human virtue, which includes the capacity to tolerate not always getting our own ways.

THE DEFECTS OF REASON

Further, conservatism has historically been suspicious of rationality untethered to political or moral tradition. This matters because rationality is the standard by which judicial engagement would evaluate laws against an underlying inclination to protect the individual's rights. The reason for conservative suspicion is twofold: first, our propensity to make mistakes with unintended consequences—that is, we, even the judges among us, are rarely as clever as we think, especially with respect to assessing the long-range consequences of our choices—and second, reason's particular tendency to become intoxicated with itself.

The first issue, the propensity for mistakes, is of course an inescapable aspect of the human condition. But it is especially amplified in politics because of the complexity of evaluating choices involving human beings living in society, combined with the temptations of power. To choose for just one person is difficult; to forecast consequences of a course of action that entails millions of people interacting in a social environment is nigh impossible. Aristotle and Burke alike teach that the accumulated wisdom of those millions, especially deployed over time, is far likelier to be wise than the judgments of even the wisest person at a given moment. The second issue, reason's capacity to get carried away with itself, is important not just because it leads to errant judgments but ultimately because it risks abusive ones. The rights of the unreasonable or irrational—those who refuse to get with the program—tend to be trampled before the armies of reason.

This classically conservative concern with the excesses of reason is not, it must be emphasized, an opposition to theory as such. It is an objection to theory loosed from circumstance. Burke bridges the two, and significantly, he says it is jurisprudence that does the bridging: "[T]he science of jurisprudence, the pride of the human intellect, which, with all its defects, redundancies, and errors, is the collected reason of ages, combining the principles of original justice with the infinite variety of human concerns."[61] Burke's point is that human experience provides a forum in which theory is applied to circumstance over and over, with ideas accreting over time. He thus speaks of "preserving the method of nature in the conduct of the state," such that "in what we improve, we are never wholly new; in what we retain we are never wholly obsolete."

OBLIGATION AND AMERICANS

To be sure, Americans are not obliged to the politics of Aristotle, Tocqueville, or Burke. We can, however, see them as sources of wisdom on which we draw to formulate an understanding of the politics of obligation and why an unchecked judiciary opposes it. Judicial engagement is hostile to the politics of obligation in multiple senses. First, individuals who seek the Court's relief rather than pursuing claims of policy or rights through the political process are deprived of the interactive, social activity—the political activity—that thinkers like Aristotle and Tocqueville argued were essential to human meaning. Whittington appears to doubt the possibility of a serious recovery of politics because so many meaningful political activities, such as jury service and lobbying, are matters we seek to avoid or outsource to hired guns. But these are not unreasonable responses to the ascendance of the judiciary, which surely does not explain them in whole but just as certainly aggravates them. If judges dispense justice, serving on a jury seems less political and more tedious. Juries in the early republic, by contrast, were active players in legal interpretation. Judicial supremacy also discourages both the winners and losers in what might otherwise be the political activity of citizens: Those who lose feel the outcome was illegitimate, and as Tocqueville observes, the perceived legitimacy of power is what rescues the rulers and the ruled from the shared indignity of oppression. Those who win are spared the hard but also rewarding work of organizing and persuasion. We are released from responsibility at the same time we are denied authority.

A theory of judicial engagement rooted in presentism deprives us of the virtue, for it is that, of fulfilling obligations. Judicial engagement generally aspires to such a fulfillment but can provide no account for it that transcends contemporary taste. Yet the connections to our past and our future enrich our lives as surely as our connections in the present, and there is something particularly honorable about faithfully discharging a debt to those who are not present to collect it. Judges are bound to precedent, which is a form of obligation to the past. But many of the New Originalists doubt even that much, preferring our contemporary judgments of constitutionality even to those that have withstood a test of time and generational consent. The virtue of humility has no place here.

Judicial engagement's innate suspicion of any common endeavor that entails coercion, which is to say any public endeavor at all, deprives us of the opportunity to build connections to one another through political activity. Even if that activity opposes coercive action, the libertarian would achieve it through nonpolitical means: judicial engagement would simply have the learned judge impose it, denying the people, finally, the dignity of being responsible for their actions, including their errors. This is a jurisprudence rooted in the Hobbesian politics of isolation and loneliness. It is also, as we shall now see, foreign to the Framers, to whom our obligation is deepest.

3. Madison's Judges

I have always thought that a construction of the instrument ought to be favoured, as far as the text would warrant, which would obviate the dilemma of a Judicial rencounter.[1]

—James Madison

In 1821, Judge Spencer Roane issued a broadside against the Marshall Court, a newspaper essay whose conclusions he apparently felt his fellow Virginian James Madison would share. Deriding the Supreme Court's decision in *Cohens v. Virginia*, which had asserted the Supreme Court's authority to review state court decisions when violations of the federal Constitution were alleged, Roane, writing in the *Richmond Enquirer* under the suggestive pseudonym "Algernon Sidney," claimed that Chief Justice John Marshall's doctrine of federal judicial supremacy over state courts in constitutional cases would decimate the states as political communities. *Cohens* was, he said, "the zenith of despotic power."[2]

Roane shared his essays with Madison, whose two replies in May and June 1821 help to illuminate the latter's view of both the nature of the union and the authority of its courts. We shall consider these in detail, but what is striking is Madison's desire—despite his view of the union as a compact not between states but between their peoples, and his defense of the Supreme Court's authority to litigate cases involving federalism—to avoid the judiciary altogether. "I have always thought," he wrote of the Constitution, "that a construction of the instrument ought to be favoured, as far as the text would warrant, which would obviate the dilemma of a Judicial rencounter." Two assumptions are pregnant in this statement. One is that construing the Constitution is not the duty of the courts alone: Madison believed, on the contrary, that a "construction" that both preceded and precluded judicial involvement was preferable to one that necessitated it. This is not the language of judicial engagement. The second is that far from being a natural or even indispensable characteristic of republican regimes, judicial resolution of fundamental questions presented a "dilemma." Madison's other writings suggest that the nature of the dilemma pitted the essentially antirepublican nature of judicial authority against the need for judicial independence.

Many originalists do not regard judicial resolution of constitutional questions as a dilemma anymore, but they stand at odds with the Madisonian legacy. This chapter will consider this view of the judiciary—and what judicial engagement sees as its paramount instrument, the Bill of Rights, augmented by the Fourteenth Amendment—through the eyes of Madison as well as other Framers. Madison is not the only Framer whose views matter. Among that distinguished group, James Wilson arguably explicated the most fully theorized view of the judiciary's role. Marshall, who participated in the ratification but not the framing of the Constitution, did far more to establish judicial authority and norms. But Madison occupies a unique role as both the foremost theorist of constitutional structure and as the statesman most responsible for the Bill of Rights. Madison's views of both how the Constitution should be interpreted and who should do the interpreting demand a reckoning. Yet that reckoning places advocates of judicial engagement in an odd position. They are originalists whose views of judicial authority and the primacy of individual rights are at least in tension with, if not in outright opposition to, those of the Framer known, with some exaggeration but also considerable justice, as the father of the Constitution.

REPUBLICANISM AND RIGHTS

We begin with Madison's commitment to republicanism and its compatibility with his theory of rights. These are often today placed at loggerheads—majority rule threatens individual rights, the account holds—but Madison saw no such incongruity. As we shall see, this is the case even where majorities behave abusively. There are, so to speak, two axes along which Madison's views require consideration. One is how a political community makes decisions, while the second is how the justice of those decisions is evaluated. The failure to separate these axes substantially confuses Madison's views. As I have elsewhere argued at greater length, Madison's republicanism was unalloyed.[3] There is no case of which I am aware in which Madison opposed the authority of a persistent majority to prevail in a political dispute. This includes cases in which Madison felt the majority was behaving unjustly. What we must strive to understand is that, unless republicanism is inherently and irredeemably prone to the abuse of political minorities—something Madison never asserted but rather, on the contrary, refuted—it is entirely consistent, once we see them as operating on different axes, to endorse majority rule while believing majorities sometimes behave unjustly. As Madison wrote, "the abuse of a trust does not disprove its existence."[4] This is no different from, for instance, defending Congress's power to declare war or to tax and spend, but also believing it sometimes abuses the authority. For Madison, the point was to arrange political institutions so as to make majoritarian abuse unlikely.

This compatibility is most evident in the very passages in which Madison is typically read as most hostile to the power of majorities. In 1786, Madison believed a treaty John Jay concluded between the United States and Spain bargained away Westerners' access to the Mississippi in favor of concessions for the Eastern states. He wrote to James Monroe:

> The progression which a certain measure [the Jay-Gardoqui Treaty] seems to be making is an alarming proof of the predominance of temporary and partial interests over those just & extended maxims of policy which have been so much boasted of among us and which alone can effectuate the durable prosperity of the Union. Should the measure triumph under the patronage of 9 States or even of the whole thirteen, I shall never be convinced that it is expedient, because I cannot conceive it to be just. There is no maxim in my opinion which is more liable to be misapplied, and which therefore more needs elucidation than the current one that the interest of the majority is the political standard of right and wrong. Taking the

word "interest" as synonimous [*sic*] with "Ultimate happiness," in which sense it is qualified with every necessary moral ingredient, the proposition is no doubt true. But taking it in the popular sense, as referring to immediate augmentation of property and wealth, nothing can be more false. In the latter sense it would be the interest of the majority in every community to despoil & enslave the minority of individuals; and in a federal community to make a similar sacrifice of the minority of the component States.[5]

The passage does indeed seem to pit majority rule against minority rights, which is how commentators have long understood it. Importantly, though, the apparent problem is the *immediacy* of majority rule, which causes the majority to mistake its "Ultimate happiness." Happiness, we note again, has an Aristotelian bearing: it is "qualified with every necessary moral ingredient," such that what is unjust cannot be expedient. But Madison here does no more than counsel majorities not to act on their instantaneous appetites—note that the treaty is not only "partial" but also "temporary"—which he will later propose constitutional mechanisms to discourage.[6] Nothing in this passage questions the *legitimacy* of majority rule or suggests any other mechanism for making decisions. It merely says majorities can be wrong.

Such is also the case in another passage often invoked to question Madison's commitment to majority rule. In his 1785 "Memorial and Remonstrance,"[7] which opposed Patrick Henry's attempt to procure public support for "teachers of the Christian religion," Madison wrote: "True it is, that no other rule exists, by which any question which may divide a Society, can be ultimately determined, but the will of the majority; but it is also true, that the majority may trespass on the rights of the minority." The key word is "also," which separates the axes of authority and justice. Madison emphatically endorses majority rule *and* says majority rule can be unjust. Nothing about the one assertion undercuts the other so long as we understand the mechanism and evaluation of public decisions on different axes. Indeed, Madison proceeds in the "Memorial and Remonstrance" to say opponents of Henry's measure would, in the case of defeat, acquiesce in the decision of the legislature and seek to change its mind in the future. He never contemplates turning to the courts despite religious freedom being already by that point enshrined in Virginia's Bill of Rights.

Nor did he in the case of the Alien and Sedition Acts, the latter of which Madison believed flagrantly to violate the First Amendment. To be sure, the Federalist-dominated courts would have provided scant relief, but it is significant that it does not seem to have occurred to anyone to ask the judiciary to declare the Act flatly unconstitutional, as opposed to convincing individual juries to nullify it by their verdicts and the public to undo it by their votes. Madison later wrote to Roane:

> Nor do I think that Congress, even seconded by the Judicial power, can without some great change in the character of the nation, succeed in durable violations of the rights & authorities of the States. The responsibility of one branch to the people, and of the other to the Legislatures of the States, seem to be, in the present stage at least of our political history, an adequate barrier. In the case of the Alien & Sedition laws, which violated the sense as well as the rights of the States, the usurping experiment was crushed at once, notwithstanding the co-operation of the federal Judges with the federal laws.

Observe that Madison says violations of rights will not be "durable." They will occur. I have elsewhere called this "quantum constitutionalism": the Constitution does not guarantee just results in individual cases but does generate higher and higher probabilities, increasing with the span of time considered, that rights will be protected.[8] The constitutional solution to which he refers was achieved at the polls in the election of 1800 in spite of judges, not because of them.

Later, in his retirement, Madison opposed the constitutionality of the Missouri Compromise on the grounds that it placed potential new states under a disability the original ones did not face. Yet, again writing to Roane, Madison neither denied the legitimacy of the majority's right to act nor sought judicial recourse. On the contrary:

But what is to controul Congress when backed & even pushed on by a majority of their Constituents, as was the case in the late contest relative to Missouri, and as may again happen in the constructive power relating to Roads & Canals? *Nothing within the pale of the Constitution* but sound arguments and conciliatory expostulations addressed both to Congress & to their constituents.[9]

In other words, it was up to aggrieved minorities to persuade a popular majority of the justice of the former's views through republican mechanisms, something the slowing of those mechanisms to encourage deliberation would facilitate. Madison notes that a sufficiently aggrieved minority can act *outside* the Constitution—that is, by rebellion, something he clearly opposes in all but the most extraordinary cases—but inside its forms; there is no alternative to majority rule. This is precisely the point he had made in the "Memorial and Remonstrance," and one he made as well to Jefferson in 1825: "The will of the nation being omnipotent for right, is so for wrong also; and the will of the nation being in the majority, the minority must submit to that danger of oppression as an evil infinitely less than the danger to the whole nation from a will independent of it."[10] This latter reference to an independent will sounds very much like how we discuss the Supreme Court today. Later, discussing the constitutionality of the Tariff of 1828, which he supported, Madison urged outraged states to recognize that even if the tariff authority had been abused, that did not mean it rose to the level of a usurpation. Abuse alone "cannot be regarded as a breach of the fundamental compact, till it reaches a degree of oppression, so iniquitous and intolerable as to justify civil war."[11]

MAJORITY ABUSE AND GOVERNMENTAL TYRANNY

Before proceeding to Madison's views of the judiciary and its role in protecting rights, there is another distinction to which we must attend. On Madison's account, the abuse of the people by the government and the abuse of the people by each other were wholly different phenomena. This distinction is absolutely central to Madison's thought, which is rendered incoherent without it. Witness James MacGregor Burns's accusation of antidemocratic tendencies in Madison's thought given that *Federalist* no. 10 announces a solution to the problem of majority abuse but *Federalist* no. 51 proceeds to place further barriers before majorities.[12] As George W. Carey has shown, the two essays are concerned with entirely different problems: One (*Federalist* no. 10) deals with some of the people abusing other of the people. The other (*Federalist* no. 51) deals with the people's exposure to arbitrary and therefore tyrannical rule.[13] Halfway through *Federalist* no. 51, Madison makes this distinction explicit: "It is of great importance in a republic, not only to guard the society against the oppression of its rulers; but to guard one part of the society against the injustice of the other part." He proceeds to the latter problem, majoritarian abuse:

> If a majority be united by a common interest, the rights of the minority will be insecure. There are but two methods of providing against this evil: the one, by creating a will in the community independent of the majority, that is, of the society itself; the other, by comprehending in the society so many separate descriptions of citizens, as will render an unjust combination of a majority of the whole very improbable, if not impracticable.

Here Madison's belief in the inevitability of majority rule is manifest: if an abusive majority unites, the minority "will be" exposed. The key is to prevent the abusive majority from uniting. Madison gives us two options for doing so. The one he dismisses, crucially, entails "creating a will in the community independent of the majority." He refers to the British royal veto, but as we shall see in chapter 4, this very conception is also the calling card of those who turn to the extrarepublican institution of the Supreme Court to protect against violations of rights. The second, which he endorses, involves a reprise of the extended-republic theory of *Federalist* no. 10, an essay that, not incidentally, proclaims a solution to the problem of majority abuse without resorting to the judiciary or to any other specific constitutional mechanism—only to the natural conditions of an extended republic.[14] This belies the idea of the courts as a countermajoritarian institution.

This distinction between governmental tyranny and abusive majorities enables us better to understand a famous passage in which Madison, introducing the Bill of Rights, seemed to empower the courts to give his amendments force:

> If they are incorporated into the constitution, independent tribunals of justice will consider themselves in a peculiar manner the guardians of those rights; they will be an impenetrable bulwark against every assumption of power in the legislative or executive; they will be naturally led to resist every encroachment upon rights expressly stipulated for in the constitution by the declaration of rights.

The question the passage presents is less whether the courts have a role in protecting rights—clearly they do—than *against whom* that authority is arrayed. The courts will be a "bulwark" against encroachments by "the legislative or executive": in other words, a barrier for the people against the elected branches of government in, we recall, cases "of a judiciary nature"; that is, those that naturally come before judges in the performance of their duties. This is the problem of governmental tyranny, not majority abuse, and the identifying mark of tyranny is arbitrary government. The courts' role is to assure the government follows the rule of law in operating on the community. What Madison never says is that the job of the courts is to protect minorities against majorities, which, as we have seen, was a distinct problem he felt the extended-republic thesis of *Federalist* no. 10 had solved without resort to institutions.[15]

On the contrary, Madison earlier in the speech drew exactly the distinction he later assumed in the passage on the judiciary. In the state constitutions, he said, some provisions of bills of rights acted against the executive, some acted against the legislative, and some acted "against the community itself; or, in other words, against the majority in favor of the minority." Recall that it was the first two of these provisions—abuse by the executive or legislative—that the judiciary could control. How, then, to handle the latter? While bills of rights amounted to a mere "paper barrier . . . yet, as they have a tendency to impress some degree of respect for them, to establish the public opinion in their favor, and to rouse the attention of the whole community, it may be one mean to controul the majority from those acts to which they might be otherwise inclined." In other words, the Bill of Rights' function in the case of majoritarian abuse was to serve as a pedagogical device that facilitated appeals back to the majority itself. Yet we cannot help but notice in this context that the vast proportion of prohibitions in the Bill of Rights are directed not against majorities but rather against the executive or, indeed, judicial branches. The judiciary will protect the people against executive or legislative abuse in the ordinary course of cases that come before them, such as the Fifth Amendment's prohibition of takings or the Sixth's entitlement to trial by jury. Only the First Amendment specifies that it prevents the passage of laws by the Congress.

THE MADISONIAN DILEMMA

Robert Bork, certainly no proponent of judicial engagement, nonetheless elucidated a "Madisonian dilemma" according to which neither majorities nor minorities could be trusted to balance popular and individual rights and that control was therefore transferred to "a nonpolitical institution," that is, the judiciary.[16] Bork took his bearings from Alexander Bickel's "counter-majoritarian difficulty."[17] But if this is a dilemma, it is not Madisonian. Madison understood some instances of majority abuse to be inevitable, but there is no instance in which he sought to resolve them by appeal to a nonpolitical institution. On the contrary, as we have seen, his solution was appeal to the majority itself, under institutional and empirical circumstances conducive to deliberation.

What then *was* Madison's theory of constitutional interpretation?

We have seen what it was not: namely, resort to extrarepublican mechanisms. The answer, as we shall now see, is that Madison was a public-meaning originalist whose exegetical approach was rooted in the Philadelphia Constitution but who nonetheless prioritized the "public" dimension over the "original" one. Moreover, he saw the meaning of the Constitution accreting from gradual precedents, including those set by the elected branches, not from instantaneous and abstract proclamations of the courts.

The only sense in which the judiciary was supreme for Madison was temporal: in the natural sequence of interpretation, it pronounced last. But for Madison, this was not only a fact but also a problem. Commenting on Jefferson's draft of a constitution for Virginia, Madison wrote in October 1788:

> In the State Constitutions & indeed in the Fedl. one also, no provision is made for the case of a disagreement in expounding them; and as the Courts are generally the last in making their decision, it results to them, by refusing or not refusing to execute a law, to stamp it with its final character. This makes the Judiciary Dept paramount in fact to the Legislature, which was never intended, and can never be proper.[18]

During Congress's 1793 debate on the removal power of the president, some members argued that the question was constitutional and thus up to the courts to decide. Madison disagreed:

> But the great objection drawn from the source to which the last arguments would lead us is, that the legislature itself has no right to expound the constitution; that wherever its meaning is doubtful, you must leave it to take its course, until the judiciary is called upon to declare its meaning. I acknowledge, in the ordinary course of government, that the exposition of the laws and constitution devolves upon the judicial. But, I beg to know, upon what principle it can be contended, that any one department draws from the

constitution greater powers than another, in marking out the limits of the powers of the several departments. The constitution is the charter of the people to the government; it specifies certain great powers as absolutely granted, and marks out the departments to exercise them. If the constitutional boundary of either be brought into question, I do not see that any one of these independent departments has more right than another to declare their sentiments on that point.[19]

To be sure, Madison does acknowledge the interpretive authority of the courts in the ordinary "course," in which case, as we have just seen, the judiciary naturally pronounces last. But this does not apply to separation of powers cases or, indeed, to others concerning the authority of each branch. The reason stems from the Constitution's source in "the people," who have allocated certain powers to each branch, each of which has interpretive power equal to the others. The separation of powers was to be maintained not by the discrete rulings of courts but rather by the mechanics of the whole system—which mechanics were why Alexander Hamilton's *Federalist* no. 84 announced that the main body of the Constitution was itself a bill of rights.[20]

In his Virginia Report, an apologia for the Virginia Resolutions' call for interposition against the Alien and Sedition laws, Madison denied that the judiciary's authority to decide legal questions proscribed what he now claimed was merely the state assembly's attempt to influence public opinion on the subject. "However true therefore it may be that the Judicial Department, is, in all questions submitted to it by the forms of the constitution, to decide in the last resort, this resort must necessarily be deemed the last in relation to the authorities of those other departments of the government; not in relation to the rights of the parties to the constitutional compact."[21] In other words, the authority of the people remained paramount.

During his presidency, Madison similarly wrote to Jefferson as the latter faced a lawsuit concerning his exercise of official duties. Madison was dubious that the judiciary would permit the suit because it would make the courts functionally superior to the executive: "In a Govt. whose vital principle, is responsibility, it never will be allowed that the Legislative & Executive Depts. should be completely subjected to the Judiciary, in which that characteristic principle is so faintly seen."[22] Writing to Edward Everett in 1830, a missive that was printed in the *North American Review,* Madison "conce[ded] power to the Supreme Court, *in cases falling within the course of its functions,*" but hastened to add that it was equally true that "the power has not always been rightly exercised."[23]

CONSTITUTIONALISM BY SETTLED PRACTICE

The result of involving all three branches in interpretation was that the meaning of the Constitution would have to be settled by practice over time. *Federalist* no. 37 explained that it was impossible to delineate the exact boundaries between the three branches of government and that the question would have to be settled by sustained practice: "All new laws, though penned with the greatest technical skill, and passed on the fullest and most mature deliberation, are considered as more or less obscure and equivocal, until their meaning be liquidated and ascertained by a series of particular discussions and adjudications."[24] Madison followed this practice when, as president, he dropped his longstanding constitutional objections to a national bank. Continued constitutional disputation on the subject was, he wrote, "precluded in my judgment by repeated recognitions under varied circumstances of the validity of such an institution in acts of the legislative, executive, and judicial branches of the Government, accompanied by indications, in different modes, of a concurrence of the general will of the nation."[25] Repeated practice that had been continually endorsed could settle constitutional questions. That did not, to be sure, change constitutional meaning. The ability of the people to change the Constitution's meaning itself even through sustained consensus would pose serious problems for originalism. On such an account, for example, the New Deal regime would be rendered literally constitutional rather than merely representing a longstanding constitutional settlement. So, as Richard Epstein notes, would judicial supremacy, a "prescriptive" result he emphatically endorses as necessary to the constitutional regime.[26] Rather, Madison's method pertained not to meaning itself but rather to the manner of settling disputes over it: that is, slowly and only on the basis of accumulated precedent. It would, he argued later in defending the constitutionality of the Tariff of 1828, be preposterous otherwise:

> A construction of the Constitution practised upon or acknowledged for a period, of nearly forty years, has received a national sanction not to be reversed, but by an evidence at least equal to the National will. If every new Congress were to disregard a meaning of the instrument uniformly sustained by their predecessors, for such a period, there would be less stability in that fundamental law, than is required for the public good, in the ordinary expositions of law.[27]

It bears remarking that the sustained interpretation in this case is Congress's, not the courts', and that constantly revolving interpretations by the legislature would undermine the stability of the Constitution "in the ordinary expositions of law"—a formulation strongly suggesting those expositions were not the judiciary's exclusive province. Far from it: discouraging the "heresy" of nullification, Madison identified a series of escalating options for redressing grievances about rights. None of these specifies the courts, and all of them are majoritarian: "The first remedy is the checks provided among the constituted authorities; that failing the next is the influence of the Ballot-boxes & Hustings; that again failing, the appeal lies to the power that made the Constitution, and can explain, amend, or remake it." This last reference can only be to the people in their constitutive capacity, and it includes the power to "explain" the law.

Madison vetoed the Bonus Bill on his last day in office because the people had not spoken on internal improvements with a sustained voice as they had on the bank. He later wrote to Monroe: "As a precedent, the case is evidently without the weight allowed to that of the National

Bank which had been often a subject of solemn discussion in Congs.[,] had long engaged the critical attention of the public, and had received reiterated & deliberate sanctions of *every* branch of the Govt., to all of which had been superadded many positive concurrences of the States, and implied ones by the people at large." Even so, Madison noted that he had proposed a Council of Revision in Philadelphia that would have involved the judiciary in bills before they became law, thus retaining the supremacy of the legislative body and resolving the republican problem posed by the judiciary pronouncing last in sequence. After all, the judiciary could not be the ultimate guardian of the Constitution, if only because not all constitutional questions would come before the courts. "These considerations remind me of the attempts in the Convention to vest in the Judiciary Dept. a qualified negative on Legislative *bills*. Such a Controul, restricted to Constitutional points, besides giving greater stability & system to the rules of expounding the Instrument, would have precluded the question of a Judiciary annulment of Legislative *Acts*."[28]

Madison's protodepartmentalism does not yet settle the question of how he himself would interpret the instrument as a constitutional actor inside one of those departments. Madison's theory of constitutional meaning itself emerged most clearly in his opposition to the original bank bill in 1791. Here Madison elucidated comprehensive standards of constitutional exegesis that partake of a legal but also prudential character. "An interpretation that destroys the very characteristic of the government"—that is, as one of only enumerated powers—"cannot be just." When the Constitution's meaning was clear, he continued, "the consequences, whatever they may be, are to be admitted—where doubtful, it is fairly triable by its consequences." Where the issue was controverted, "the meaning of the parties to the instrument" —this as opposed to the *drafters* of the instrument—"if to be collected by reasonable evidence, is a proper guide." This is the foundation of public-meaning originalism: the Constitution's original meaning is to be ascertained not by reference to the private intentions of its drafters but rather according to the public understanding of those who ratified it. "Cotemporary and concurrent expositions are a reasonable evidence of the meaning of the parties."[29]

Finally, he addressed claims that the authority for a bank could be implicit: "In admitting or rejecting a constructive authority, not only the degree of its incidentality to an express authority, is to be regarded, but the degree of its importance also; since on this will depend the probability or improbability of its being left to construction." This last standard is especially revealing, because the importance of an implied power was a prudential question of a type to which Madison believed the courts were incompetent. Later, in his Bonus Bill veto, Madison said questions of "policy and expedience [were] unsuspectible of judicial cognizance and action."[30]

Epstein's argument for judicial supremacy via the doctrine of long usage presents other difficulties. On Madison's own account, there is a sense in which he is right, which is that judicial review as used in *Marbury v. Madison* and judicial authority to impose the Supremacy Clause as decided in *Martin v. Hunter's Lessee* seem difficult to dislodge. But they do not establish judicial supremacy in constitutional interpretation over the other branches of government, only a power of judicial review on the part of the courts that includes federal supremacy over decisions of state courts. Neither case establishes a doctrine of judicial *finality* over constitutional questions generally, nor does either inhibit the political branches of the national government from arriving at their own constitutional views. Perhaps the most important response is that prescriptive practice is an ongoing process. To the extent—which is doubtful at best and positively disprovable at worst—that settled practice entails full-scale judicial engagement, it can be unsettled. Prescription merely requires that the process occur in slow and deliberate steps.

FEDERALISM AND THE COURTS

There was one area in which Madison, with reasonable consistency, held that the judiciary power was supreme: cases of disputes between state and national authority, a power that arose from the Supremacy Clause of Article VI. *Federalist* no. 39 had explained:

It is true, that in controversies relating to the boundary between the two jurisdictions, the tribunal which is ultimately to decide, is to be established under the general government. But this does not change the principle of the case. The decision is to be impartially made, according to the rules of the constitution: and all the usual and most effectual precautions are taken to secure this impartiality. Some such tribunal is clearly essential to prevent an appeal to the sword, and a dissolution of the compact; and that it ought to be established under the general, rather than under the local governments; or, to speak more properly, that it could be safely established under the first alone, is a position not likely to be combated.[31]

As Carey has shown, this model of "constitutional federalism"—that is, the judiciary deciding questions of state-national relations with regard to the fixed rules of the Constitution—is at odds with Madison's nearly simultaneous argument in *Federalist* no. 46 that the "common constituents" of the state and national governments would settle these questions.[32] This opposition between constitutional and "political" federalism can be resolved, if at all, only when we recall that Madison believed the ultimate authority for judicial decisions came from public approval of them. Madison would later specify that the model of judicial supremacy over questions of federalism he elucidated in *Federalist* no. 39 represented his enduring view. He wrote in 1829 that, except in usurpations of state authority so extreme as to warrant the extraconstitutional step of rebellion, "there is an Arbiter or Umpire, as within the Governments of the States, so within that of the U.S. in the authority constitutionally provided for deciding, controversies concerning boundaries of right and power. The provision in the U.S. is particularly stated in the Federalist, No. 39."[33] The reason, he separately explained, was that it was only just that disputes between parts and the whole be adjudicated by the whole. What Madison never held was that the federal judiciary was supreme over matters purely internal to federal governance.

It is in this context that we can best understand Madison's correspondence with Roane. His first dispatch, in May 1821, "regretted that the Court is so much in the practice of mingling with the Judgments pronounced, comments & reasonings of a scope beyond them; and that in these there is often an apparent disposition to amplify the authorities of the Union, at the expence of those of the States." The first point, regarding Marshall's propensity to declare the meaning of the Constitution in the abstract rather than confining himself to the immediate dispute between the parties at the bar, speaks to Madison's judicial minimalism: the Court should not decide more than necessary, nor should it do so on a wider basis than necessary, a point reinforced by his separate advocacy of seriatim opinions as a means of lessening the force of precedent.[34]

Madison proceeded to say he was less concerned about the jurisdiction the judiciary had claimed for itself vis-à-vis the state courts than he was with "the latitude of power which it has assigned to the Legislature." This reference to the judiciary "assign[ing]" power to the Congress suggests the Court has *asserted* a right to police legislative powers. Madison does not here explicitly approve the assertion. In any event, we have already seen Madison say other branches shared a coordinate right to do so as well. Corresponding with Jefferson in 1824, Madison described judicial review of federalism cases as the only alternative to an appeal to the sword. The significant fact is that Madison explicitly distinguished the federalism case from those involving separation of powers within the federal government. "In the latter case neither party being able to consummate its will without the concurrence of the other, there is a necessity on both to consult and to accommodate."[35] It was only in the federalism case that Madison relied on judicial resolution. The alternative there was a "trial of strength." The separation of powers, not the discrete power of the courts, was the solution to excesses of legislative authority.

In the May 1821 letter to Roane, Madison specified that these structural and political factors would control the Congress while, importantly, there were ample constitutional means for keeping the judiciary in its power as well. These included the impeachability of judges, which *Federalist* no. 81 had suggested was a tool available for errant rulings. Madison wrote Roane: "It is not probable that the Supreme Court would be long indulged in a career of usurpation opposed to the decided opinions & policy of the Legislature." "Long" here is suggestive. Like any constitutional authority, judicial power is subject to temporary but not sustained abuse. The same is true of the Congress. As we have already seen, Congress could not "succeed in durable violations" of the Constitution because one branch of it was responsible to the states and the other to the people. If, again, it did succeed—as it had in the Missouri Compromise—there was no *constitutional* solution but appeal to the people. Madison did not mention the judiciary as a final arbiter here. The best it could do was help require congressional decisions to be "durable" before they prevailed.

Madison was not worried, he told Roane, about *Cohens'* assertion of judicial authority over cases originating in the state courts. The reason is important. "[T]here is as yet no evidence they express either the opinions of Congress, or those of their Constituents." If Congress did oppose decisions of the Court that augmented federal power, they could choose either not to exercise the powers or, significantly, to "find the means of controuling those [powers] claimed by the Court for itself." As always, if Congress acted wrongly, its constituents were empowered to "effectuate a compliance with their deliberate judgment & settled determination." Again we see that the public will, like the legislature's, must be "deliberate" and "settled" before it prevails.

That is not to say the judiciary had no role in confining federal powers, a question complicated by the extent of the enumerated power over the federal capital district, one of the issues at stake in *Cohens.* The Necessary and Proper Clause was "subjoined" to this authority, thus widening it. "All that could be exacted however by these considerations would be, that the means of execution should be of the most obvious & essential kind." To the extent the issue of federal control of the capital was unclear—which Madison believed it might be with respect to the federal district's relationship with state laws—it would be best to resolve the issue with a constitutional amendment.

As to "legal precedents"—by which, interestingly, Madison meant laws passed by Congress, not decisions of the courts—"the distinction should ever be strictly attended to, between such as take place under transitory impressions, or without full examination & deliberation, and such as pass with solemnities & repetitions, sufficient to imply a concurrence of the judgment & the will of those who having granted the power have the ultimate right to explain the grant." That is, the ultimate interpretive power lay with the people, not the courts. "The Judicial power of the U.S. over cases arising under the Constitution," he continued, "must be admitted to be a vital part of the system." But it was subject to "limits and exceptions" whose scope remained unclear. "A liberal and steady course of practice alone can reconcile the several provisions of the Constitution literally at variance with one another." At a minimum, even in federal cases, the judiciary should only issue decisions "touch[ing] individuals" as opposed to the states as corporate bodies since the latter could not, as a practical matter, be coerced.

In his second letter to Roane, in June 1821, Madison made his argument for avoiding the "dilemma of a Judicial reencounter," but specified that "on the abstract question of whether the federal, or the State decisions ought to prevail, the sounder policy would yield to the claims of the former." Still, this question was "abstract," one of constitutional philosophy generally, and we have already seen that abstract questions, as opposed to concrete controversies, were not judicial matters. Madison specified, against Roane, that the Union was not a compact between the states as corporate entities but rather one between their peoples. Controversies were better referred to "the Government representing the whole and exercised by its tribunals." But Madison offered this reassurance: "Is it not a reasonable calculation also that the room for jarring opinions between the national & State Tribunals will be narrowed by successive decisions sanctioned by the public concurrence," and that the state courts would become weightier as they improved structurally. One improvement would be decisions that "at once indicat[ed] & influenc[ed] the sense of their Constituents." Public opinion was ultimately to prevail. We now turn to the question of why, and what the answer says about judicial engagement.

MADISON AND MAJORITIES

In 1835, Madison composed an unaddressed letter—apparently intended as a memorandum to work out his own thoughts on the subject—on "majority governments." The doctrine of majority governments as oppressive "strikes at the root of Republicanism, and if pursued into its consequences, must terminate in absolute monarchy, with a standing military force; such alone being impartial between its subjects, and alone capable of overpowering majorities as well as minorities." Again, despite the fact that majoritarian abuse is a central concern of advocates of judicial engagement, we see no mention of the judiciary as an "impartial" entity here. Instead, Madison paraphrased his extended-republic thesis as the best security against majoritarian abuse. Abuses were likelier inside states, which were smaller, and one solution was giving "an appellate supremacy to the Judicial department of the U.S.," an apparent reference, again, to state majorities encroaching on federal jurisdiction. Madison then cut to the heart of the issue:

> It has been said that all Govt. is an evil. It wd. be more proper to say that the necessity of any Govt. is a misfortune. This necessity however exists; and the problem to be solved is, not what form of Govt. is perfect, but which of the forms is least imperfect. And here the general question between a Republican Governt. in which the majority rule the minority, and a Govt. in which a lesser number or the least number rule the majority. If the Republican form is, as all of us agree, to be preferred, the final question must be what is the structure of it, that will best guard agst. precipitate Counsels and factious combinations for unjust purposes, without a sacrifice of the fundamental principle of Republicanism. Those who denounce majority Govts altogether because they may have an interest in abusing their power, denounce at the same time all Republican Govt. and must maintain that minority Govts. would feel less of the bias of interest, or the seductions of power. . . . [I]f Majority Govts.

as such be the worst of Govts. those who think & say so can not be within the pale of the Republican faith.

Madison acknowledged that among the three branches of government "it must still be true that the Judicial most familiarize itself, to the attention of [the public] as the expositr. of Constitutional questions" both because of the sequence of its decisions and because—structurally occupying a middle ground between the unity of the executive and the plurality of the legislature—it inspired more public confidence. This public confidence remained the ultimate arbiter. Importantly, in cases in which a minority power—this perhaps included the courts—had constitutional power over a numerical majority, their power depended ultimately on the justice of their views and their ability to persuade a majority. "[T]he abuses of all other Govts. have led to the preference of Republican Govt. [as] the best of all governments because the least imperfect." The "vital principle of Repub. Govt. is the lex majoris partis, the will of the majority."

Madison's point was that the ultimate alternative to majority rule was minority rule. This is a point with which advocates of judicial engagement—and even opponents of it like Bork—must contend. True, advocates of judicial engagement might claim they promote the rule of the majorities who enacted the Constitution, but this presumes judges are the proper vehicle for doing so. We have seen that Madison provided standards of constitutional interpretation, but did so to a legislature; that he believed in a bill of rights, but not as a legal tool for protecting minorities against majorities; that judicial supremacy was confined to cases of federalism, and even then its force came from sustained public support; and that, the vital point—the Paradox of Engagement—there was no reason to believe a body exempted from accountability would be more faithful to the Constitution than one that was subject to public opinion.

Thus Madison. What of other Framers?

HAMILTON ON JUDICIAL REVIEW

Hamilton is widely and justly seen as the champion of judicial review among the Framers. This much seems irrefutable, both given the nature of a written constitution and *The Federalist's* explicit endorsement of that mechanism. Hamilton, after all, argued for judicial review in one of the young republic's first cases in which it was exercised, 1784's *Rutgers v. Waddington*.[36] But a careful reading of *Federalist* no. 78, his definitive statement on judicial review, suggests Hamilton's conception of judicial power is broadly compatible with Madison's. This essay, like Madison's writings, depends on a proper understanding of the separation of powers, which, to repeat, is directed not toward majorities but rather toward those who occupy the power of the regime at any given moment. In other words, it seeks less to control majorities, an issue *The Federalist* has long since settled in essay no. 10, than to prevent exposure to the arbitrary rule of the government.

Toward the beginning of *Federalist* no. 78, Hamilton, defending the "good behavior" standard for judicial tenure, suggests the distinction: "In a monarchy, it is an excellent barrier to the despotism of the prince: in a republic it is a no less excellent barrier to the encroachments and oppressions *of the representative body*."[37] The judiciary's job is to "secure a steady, upright, and impartial administration of the laws." In the essay's most famous passage, Hamilton says the judiciary compared to the other departments "will always be the least dangerous to the political rights of the constitution" because it has "neither FORCE nor WILL, but merely judgment; and must ultimately depend upon the aid of the executive arm even for the efficacy of its judgments." The counterposition is of "will," which evidently entails the prudential exercise of legislative discretion among a range of available alternatives, to "judgment," which, as Carey writes, "would seem to have a more passive connotation."[38] Matthew J. Franck, asserting that Hamilton's case for judicial review is "cautious," also notes that we must proceed to ask: "Least dangerous to what? To the *'political rights of the Constitution'*; that is, to the rightful prerogatives of the other branches (and conceivably to those of the states as well)."³⁹ Judges, Hamilton tells us later in the essay, do not have "arbitrary discretion"; rather, "it is indispensable that they should be bound down by strict rules and precedents, which serve to define and point out their duty in every particular case that comes before them."⁴⁰

Hamilton proceeds to explain that "though individual oppression may now and then proceed from the courts of justice, the general liberty of the people can never be endangered from that quarter: I mean, so long as the judiciary remains truly distinct from both the legislature and the executive." This passage suggests, first, that there is a difference between "individual oppression" and the "general liberty of the people," such that "the people" is more than, or at least distinct from, a collection of isolated individuals. What is the "general" liberty of the people? Apparently Hamilton refers to republican self-government, for the only way for the judiciary to endanger it is to invade the terrain of the elected branches. Liberty, indeed, would be endangered were the judiciary linked with the other departments. This distinction is fortified by Hamilton's reference later in the essay to "the rights of the constitution, *and* of individuals," suggesting there is a difference.⁴¹

Moreover, Hamilton's reference to "individuals" whom judges have the capacity, if rarely, to oppress seems to underscore Madison's assertion that the courts would have jurisdiction only over cases "of a judiciary nature." These are disputes, especially in criminal cases, involving individuals rather than abstract constitutional questions. This is borne out when Hamilton immediately explains that independent courts are especially important under a "limited constitution" that "contains certain specified exceptions to the legislative authority." His examples of these—bills of attainder and ex post facto laws—are all cases of a clearly judiciary nature, ones in which an individual would be brought before the courts or would obviously turn to them for relief. The legislative body cannot be presumed to be "the constitutional judges of their own powers," but again, he refers not to majority-minority disputes but rather to tyrannical acts committed by elected officials against the people. Indeed, this power of judicial review is necessary so that representatives do *not* "substitute their *will* to that of their constituents. It is far more rational to suppose that the courts were designed to be an intermediate body between the people and the legislature, in order, among other things, to keep the latter within the limits assigned to their authority"—limits to which he has previously referred as "exceptions" to legislative power that are justiciable in individual disputes. The Constitution, importantly, embodies "the intention of the people," which must be preferred, when in conflict, to "the intention of their agents."

Hamilton supplies a clear standard for judicial review: a law must be at "irreconcilable variance" with the Constitution before courts refuse to apply it, a kind of law that, as Lino Graglia notes, is "rarely, if ever, enacted."[42] Hamilton's phrase strongly suggests a duty of judges to attempt to reconcile a law with the Constitution: that is, a presumption of constitutionality. He similarly speaks of laws that violate not just the general but rather the "manifest" tenor of the Constitution.[43] This sounds very much like rational-basis review. Hamilton does proceed to say that judicial review is

> equally requisite to guard the constitution and the rights of individuals from the effects of those ill humours which the arts of designing men, or the influence of particular conjunctures, sometimes disseminate among the people themselves, and which, though they speedily give place to better information and more deliberate reflection, have a tendency, in the mean time, to occasion dangerous innovations in the government, and serious oppressions of the minor party in the community.[44]

This, it must be acknowledged, seems to give the judiciary some authority in cases of majority abuse. But note that Hamilton describes these instances as rare and, crucially, self-correcting, such that the judiciary's real function is to buy time. After all, he says, judges would need "an uncommon portion of fortitude" when "legislative invasions of [the Constitution] had been instigated by the major voice of the community." We are, in other words, speaking of situations that would be exceptionally unusual, and still speaking as well of cases that otherwise come before the courts in the course of their duties.

Later in the essay, Hamilton does refer to judges protecting citizens against "the effects of occasional ill humours in the society. These sometimes extend no farther than to the injury of the private rights of particular classes of citizens, by unjust and partial laws." This clearly engages the judiciary in something like protecting minorities against majorities. Justice Harlan Fiske Stone famously said that the judicial function was to help ensure that laws represented the "sober second thought of the community, which is the firm base on which all law must ultimately rest."[45] Yet Hamilton clearly distinguishes this duty to deal with "unjust and partial laws" from "infractions of the constitution," referring apparently to equity, not law: judges will "mitigate[e] the severity and confin[e] the operation of such laws."[46] He does not say they will void them. Moreover, he proceeds to associate this function again with a check on the legislature vis-à-vis the people: "It not only serves to moderate the immediate mischiefs of those [laws] which may have been passed, but it operates as a check on the legislative body in passing them; who, perceiving that obstacles to the success of an iniquitous intention are to be expected from the scruples of the courts, are in a manner compelled, by the very motives of the injustice they meditate, to qualify their attempts." In other words, Hamilton says an underappreciated function of judicial review is not to void laws but rather to discourage their passage by introducing questions of justice into legislative deliberation.

There is little gainsaying the fact that Hamilton's view of judicial authority is broad, but there is no basis here for seeing the judges as superintendents of the justice or rightness of laws generally, an authority some proponents of judicial engagement import into the Constitution through such terms as "due process of law." On the contrary, almost contemporaneously with the Philadelphia Convention, Hamilton remarked to the New York Assembly that terms like "the law of the land" and "due process" were purely procedural, pertained to judicial procedures at that, and "can never be referred to an act of legislature."[47] This is an explicit rejection of substantive due process, especially that species of it that, as we shall see in chapter 4, would use this clause to empower judges to review whether laws are, in the Augustinian sense, really "laws" at all. Moreover, in *Federalist* no. 81, Hamilton explicitly denies that so much as "a syllable" of the Constitution licenses any appeal to "the spirit of the constitution," which had been among Brutus's concerns.

As *The Federalist* proceeds, we further find Hamilton supplying means of controlling the judiciary, especially impeachment, which he suggestively calls a "precautio[n] for their responsibility," one that will be used in cases of "mal-conduct." [48] To what does Hamilton refer? Evidently he means that impeachment is a tool for controlling judges who abuse their authority by veering outside the realm of judgment and into will. The judiciary may misconstrue the Constitution and contravene the "will" of Congress "now and then," but these occasions will "never be so extensive as to amount to an inconvenience, or in any sensible degree to affect the order of the political system." If judges do so persistently—through "a series of deliberate usurpations on the authority of the legislature"—impeachment is available. "This alone is a complete security."[49] In addition, "the national legislature will have ample authority to make such *exceptions,* and to prescribe such regulations, as will be calculated to obviate or remove" any inconveniences found that emerge in the "particular powers of the federal judiciary." Congress cannot reverse a ruling in a "particular case," but "may prescribe a new rule for future cases." [50] This would appear to be an institutional arrangement in which Congress ultimately outranks the judiciary.

CONSTITUTIONAL ARCHITECTURE

The structure and early history of the Constitution equally suggests judges were not meant to exercise ultimate control of the regime. As Akhil Reed Amar notes, the Constitution gives the other departments power to structure the Court but the Court no comparable constitutive power over the other branches. Moreover, as he also notes, the Judiciary

Act of 1789 prescribed a Supreme Court of six, an even number: "From a modern perspective that views Court opinions as the unique last word on constitutional meaning—existing on a far higher plane than the constitutional views of congressmen, presidents, jurors, and voters—the number six might seem highly dysfunctional. After all, if the justices tied three to three, the country would lack definitive guidance from its anointed oracle."[51] Even under Marshall, the Court invalidated only a single provision of federal law, confining itself mostly to policing federalism disputes. Despite Madison's claim that the National Bank had been sustained by all three branches of government, it actually did not come before the Court until 1819, and then only when it was framed as a dispute over state-national authority. The Court did not deal with the Bill of Rights extensively until the late nineteenth and early twentieth centuries. The idea of the Court as a place where constitutional complaints were presented for ultimate disposition simply finds no support in the structure or early practice of the Constitution.

INDEPENDENT OR COEQUAL?

But, say advocates of judicial engagement, the judiciary is a coequal branch of government, and, as Barnett suggests, all three branches are equally entitled to scuttle a measure.[52] David M. Burke would go even further, apparently involving the judiciary in the wisdom of laws by suggesting that the separation of powers prevents majorities from prevailing "absent a consensus among the three independent, coequal, and coordinate branches of government that the law in question is wise and constitutional."[53] This idea of three "separate but equal" branches has taken hold of the popular understanding of the Constitution despite the sorry provenance of the phrase in constitutional history. But it is a linguistic sleight of hand. The Framers certainly intended some version of interdepartmental equality, though they used terms like "coordinate" and "coextensive" to describe the judiciary's relationship to the other branches—terms that more precisely connote how it corresponds to them. As David J. Siemers notes, the point was not that the branches were equal in power but rather that they were not subordinate to each other in the exercise of each one's legitimate functions.[54] It seems clear enough that the Framers cannot have meant that all three branches would have an equal share in the shaping of national policy. Otherwise Alexander Hamilton could never have said that the judiciary was "the least dangerous" branch of government. The judiciary's role is plainly derivative in some sense from the legislative. Just as James Madison wrote that that the executive power "must presuppose the existence of the laws to be executed,"[55] the judiciary power must assume an act of the elective branches to be interpreted. Furthermore, the judiciary has no power of initiation, only of reaction, and most laws are never constitutionally disputed.

As Siemers notes, the Supreme Court did not describe itself in "coequal" terms until the late nineteenth century, and even then its meaning was often that it had a duty to defer to Congress because the legislature was coequal. There are other reasons to suggest Congress was intended to operate as the First Branch. As Carey among others has observed, members of Congress have a power of impeachment and removal over the judiciary—as over the executive—yet the other branches have no comparable authority over the legislature.[56] The legislature controls the major levers of the regime; when *The Federalist* speaks of the powers of "the government," it almost always refers to the powers of Congress, using the terms nearly synonymously.[57] The only other enumerated powers under the Constitution, those of the executive, are almost all qualified by corresponding powers of Congress.

Montesquieu, the most systematic theorist of separation of powers and the one who wielded the most influence on the American Founders, spoke of "separate" powers but did not describe their influence as equal, as in: "Nor is there liberty if the power of judging is not separate from legislative power and from executive power."[58] On the contrary, he wrote that of the three powers, while the legislature had the power to make laws and the executive the power to initiate action, the power "of judging is in some fashion, null."[59] In his 1776 pamphlet "Thoughts on Government,"

John Adams seemed similarly to see the judiciary as a junior or adjunctive partner, referring to it as "hold[ing] the balance between the two contending powers," that is, the legislative and executive.[60]

The Framers referred to the judiciary in similar terms. For example, in speaking of the proposed Council of Revision in the Philadelphia Convention of 1787, Madison said the council's purpose was, among others, to "restrain the Legislature from encroaching on the other co-ordinate departments."[61] "Coordinate," to be sure, is the opposite of "subordinate," implying some equality in rank but, again, the meaning is that no branch is subordinate to another within the performance of its proper functions. In no sense does coordinateness suggest all the branches are equal in influence. This observation is bolstered by Hamilton's use of "coordinate" in *Federalist* no. 78 in the same breath in which he reiterates the idea that the judiciary is incapable of abuse because of its inherent weakness:

> [A]s liberty can have nothing to fear from the judiciary alone, but
> would have everything to fear from its union with either of the
> other departments; that as all the effects of such a union must ensue
> from a dependence of the former on the latter, notwithstanding
> a nominal and apparent separation; that as from the natural
> feebleness of the judiciary, it is in continual jeopardy of being
> overpowered, awed or influenced by its *coordinate* branches . . .[62]

In *Federalist* no. 48, Madison refers to the branches as "co-ordinate" but the legislature as having a "superiority in our governments" because its "constitutional powers [are] more extensive, and less susceptible of precise limits," enabling it to encroach on the others more easily. Encroachments by the other departments, by contrast, are clearly visible.[63] The succeeding essay, also from Madison's pen, seems to endorse something like popular constitutionalism, suggesting that because "[t]he several departments [are] perfectly co-ordinate by the terms of their common commissions, neither of them, it is evident, can pretend to an exclusive or superior right of settling the boundaries between their respective powers," such that "the people themselves . . . can alone declare [the Constitution's] true meaning."[64]

In his *Lectures on Law,* James Wilson, by then a Supreme Court justice and a muscular proponent of judicial review, also employed the term "coordinate," but again not in a context that suggested a comparable range of authority between the courts and the other branches. On the contrary, his point was that judges were not subordinate to the other branches in those areas in which they had authority:

> The judges of the United States stand on a much more independent footing than that on which the judges of England stand, with regard to jurisdiction, as well as with regard to commissions and salaries. In many cases, the jurisdiction of the judges of the United States is ascertained and secured by the constitution: *as to these,* the power of the judicial is coordinate with that of the legislative department. As to the other cases, by the necessary result of the constitution, the authority of the former is paramount to the authority of the latter.[65]

In other words, judges were coordinate in that they were independent of the other branches. St. George Tucker's connotation of the word was similar. Judges could not advise policymakers as they did in England because:

> [I]n the United States of America, the judicial power is a distinct, separate, independent, and co-ordinate branch of the government. . . . The obligation which the constitution imposes upon the judiciary department to support the constitution of the United States, would be nugatory, if it were dependent upon either of the other branches of the government, or in any manner subject to their control.[66]

In his *Commentaries on American Law,* James Chancellor Kent's understanding of "coordinate powers" is among the more assertive: Exempting the legislature from judicial review would be the equivalent of "declaring, that the will of only one concurrent and co-ordinate department of subordinate authorities under the constitution, was absolute over the other departments." Put otherwise, in this case, the legislative power is *only* coordinate and no more. Consequently, it is a "settled principle in the legal polity of this country, that it belongs to the judicial power, as a matter of right and duty, to declare every act of the legislature made in violation of the constitution, or of any provision of it, null and void," a power that, significantly, he dates to *Hayburn's Case,* not *Marbury.*[67] Yet later, Kent—emphasizing that the judicial power must be "coextensive with the power of legislation," a concept to which we shall return—assigns the courts authority as "the final expositor of the Constitution, as to all questions of a judicial nature"; that is, only as to questions of such a nature. In his edition of the *Commentaries,* Oliver Wendell Holmes added a note to qualify the statement further: "But the judicial power seems to be limited as against a co-ordinate branch of the government."[68] Kent's original echoes Madison's remark in Philadelphia about the judiciary having authority only in cases that naturally come before it.

In 1834, Madison outlined his views on the authority of the Supreme Court in interdepartmental disputes within the national government:

As the Legislative, Executive, and Judicial departments of the United States are co-ordinate, and each equally bound to support the Constitution, it follows that each must, in the exercise of its functions, be guided by the text of the Constitution according to its own interpretation of it; and, consequently, that in the event of irreconcilable interpretations, the prevalence of the one or the other department must depend on the nature of the case, as receiving its final decision from the one or the other, and passing from that decision into effect, without involving the functions of any other.[69]

This appears to endorse departmentalism on the grounds of coordinateness. Larry D. Kramer understands Madison, however, to proceed to judicial supremacy. Because constitutional questions will "generally find their ultimate discussion and operative decision" in the judiciary, and because the size of the Court occupies a sweet spot between a single executive and a "multitudinous" legislature, Madison says the public will generally defer to the Court. But this is better understood as an empirical prediction than a normative endorsement of judicial finality, which Madison makes clear by qualifying the prophecy: "Without losing sight, therefore, of the co-ordinate relations of the three branches to each other, it may always be expected that the judicial branch, when happily filled, will, for the reasons suggested, most engage the respect and reliance of the public."[70]

We may draw several conclusions from this evidence. The Founders saw the judiciary as coordinate yet inherently weaker. Yet this was not merely an empirical analysis of the judiciary: *Federalist* no. 78 indicated the courts were to invalidate a law only in a case of "irreconcilable variance" between it and the Constitution.[71] Congress, for example, is under no comparable burden to pass a law only where it is in irreconcilable compliance with the Constitution. The Court is expected to act only in a clear case. Thus, Justice Miller in the *Trade-Mark Cases:*

> We adopt this course because when this Court is called on in the course of the administration of the law to consider whether an act of Congress, or of any other department of the government, is within the constitutional authority of that department, a due respect for a co-ordinate branch of the government requires that we shall decide that it has transcended its powers only when that is so plain that we cannot avoid the duty.[72]

There is, in other words, a constitutional norm governing judicial behavior according to which judges act only in clear cases. There is dispute, to be sure, as to what would constitute clear, ranging from James Bradley Thayer's extreme deference[73] to John McGinnis's "duty of clarity."[74] This range is why Richard Posner, denying that theories of restraint supply a theory for deciding cases, can throw constitutional caution to the wind and embrace a pragmatic approach that altogether rejects theory in favor of deciding based on the effects of a ruling.[75] The important point for our purposes is that while Congress is expected to govern constitutionally, it does not operate under the same norm of restraint.

Moreover, coordinateness implies a duty of all three branches to interpret the Constitution, not for them to defer to the courts. Justice Joseph Story wrote in his *Commentaries on the Constitution* that the duty of constitutional interpretation "may arise in the course of the discharge of the functions of any one, or of all, of the great departments of government, the executive, the legislative, and the judicial. . . . And in many cases the decisions of the executive and legislative departments, thus made, become final and conclusive, being from their very nature and character incapable of revision."[76] In cases in which a tax, treaty or other similar measure raises constitutional controversy, "[t]he remedy . . . is solely by an appeal to the people at the elections; or by the salutary power of amendment, provided by the constitution itself."[77] It is only when a question is "of a different nature, and capable of judicial inquiry and decision" that it is "subject to judicial revision. It is in such cases, as we conceive, that there is a final and common arbiter provided by the constitution itself, to whose decisions all others are subordinate; and that arbiter is the supreme judicial authority of the courts of the Union."[78] These are, as we have seen, cases of a judiciary nature.

What seems clear, then, is that a decision of the Court in a realm subject to its authority is intended to be coordinate with the other departments. Michael Stokes Paulsen is correct, for example, to note that President Lincoln ignored the Court's specific order in *Merryman v. United States,* but this was a case of extraordinary power for an extreme situation, not a precedent for commonplace use.[79] But Congress plainly has the power to inhibit such a decision simply by removing jurisdiction over it. Moreover, the coordinate authority of the courts extends to their rulings in specific cases, not to the Constitution generally. *Marbury* consequently refers to judges as "[t]hose who apply the rule to particular cases."[80] The Supreme Court can, for example, assess the compatibility between the Affordable Care Act and the Commerce Clause, but the other branches are not bound to heed abstract judicial pronouncements on the Commerce Clause generally. This was the import of Lincoln's reaction to *Dred Scott,* famously expressed in his First Inaugural:

> I do not forget the position assumed by some, that constitutional questions are to be decided by the Supreme Court; nor do I deny that such decisions must be binding in any case, upon the parties to a suit, as to the object of that suit, while they are also entitled to very high respect and consideration, in all parallel cases, by all other departments of the government. . . . At the same time the candid citizen must confess that if the policy of the government, upon vital questions, affecting the whole people, is to be irrevocably fixed by decisions of the Supreme Court, the instant they are made, in ordinary litigation between parties, in personal actions, the people will have ceased, to be their own rulers, having, to that extent, practically resigned their government, into the hands of that eminent tribunal.[81]

To be sure, the Framers were a broad and diverse group. Neither Madison, Hamilton, nor Wilson can speak for them all, and it would be too much to say they converge in all particulars around the perspective on judicial power presented in this study. But it would be reasonable to say there is no basis among them for the theory of judicial engagement, to which we now turn.

4. The Antipolitical Constitution

> I am only challenging the widely held assumption that, because of popular sovereignty or the consent of the governed, "We the People" are bound in conscience to obey any law that is enacted by constitutional means. Further, because unanimous consent is never required, in practice the "consent of the governed" is reduced to the consent of a majority of legislators who are elected by a majority of those who vote in an election. In short, "We the People" is a fiction.
>
> —Randy E. Barnett[1]

Justice Felix Frankfurter was few conservatives' ideal of a judge. An ardent New Dealer who informally advised President Franklin Roosevelt while sitting on the bench, his views of judicial modesty led him to defer to Congress and the executive branch not just on a broad array of cases asserting economic rights, but also to concur in the notorious Japanese-American internment case, *Korematsu v. United States*.[2] But as we have seen, Frankfurter also holds the distinction of having been relatively consistent in his deference to the elected branches of government, such that he was increasingly perceived as a conservative when the Warren Court began its active use of judicial review for liberal purposes. Frankfurter merits our attention because of his understanding of the existence of political community rather than merely a collection of individuals. The mostly forgotten case of *McGowan v. Maryland* illustrates the point.[3]

The case concerned the state of Maryland's "blue laws," which forbade a wide array of commercial activity on Sundays. Such laws were once common in dozens of states, though they have now largely faded away or been gutted unto pointlessness. (In Massachusetts, for example, alcohol retailers must wait all the way to 10 a.m. to open on Sundays.[4]) The provenance of blue laws is self-evidently sectarian: Sunday is the sabbath of what Chief Justice Earl Warren, upholding the laws for an 8-1 Court, called "the dominant Christian sects."[5]

In *McGowan*, several employees of retailers in Anne Arundel County, Maryland, were indicted for selling forbidden goods on a Sunday. Chief Justice Warren did precisely what champions of judicial engagement say judges should not do: instead of an inquiry into the actual motives of the legislature, he hunted for a purpose that would render blue laws constitutional, concluding that "as presently written and administered, most of them, at least, are of a secular rather than of a religious character."[6] Attempting to resolve the appellants' claim that the laws were arbitrary because some goods could be sold and some could not, Warren went as far as to concoct reasons for the blue laws and then invoke a lack of evidence disproving them: "It would seem that a legislature could reasonably find that the Sunday sale of the exempted commodities was necessary either for the health of the populace or for the enhancement of the recreational atmosphere of the day. . . . The record is barren of any indication that this apparently reasonable basis does not exist, that local tradition and custom might not rationally call for this legislative treatment."[7]

There was an air of silliness about all this. Everyone knows why blue laws set Sunday, as opposed to Monday or Tuesday, apart. Moreover, putting tradition, which Warren said could "rationally" dictate blue laws, to the test of discrete reason—that is, implying that it is permissible only when reason can otherwise validate it—naturally disadvantages custom, whose premise is that Burke's "collected reason of ages" may contain wisdom not immediately apparent to the all-consuming now. Frankfurter, concurring in the Court's decision but writing separately, had the better part of the argument. He denied the possibility of investigating the motives of a legislature as though it were a single unified actor responding to identifiable political pressures: "To ask what interest, what objective, legislation serves, of course, is not to psychoanalyze legislators, but to examine the necessary effects of what they have enacted."[8] The effect of the law was to set Sundays apart as "a day of rest not merely in a physical, hygienic sense, but in the sense of a recurrent time in the cycle of human activity when the rhythms of existence changed, a day of particular associations which came to have their own autonomous value for life."[9] Perhaps more important, rather than seeing the case as one pitting lone objectors against the state, Frankfurter recognized the individual's situation in the context of a political community whose "spirit . . . expresses in goodly measure the heritage which links it to its past" and which could reasonably decide to create an "atmosphere of general repose" that would be disrupted by exempting individuals from the law.[10]

In other words, the majority of the community was entitled to impose regulations that created what it regarded as conditions for living a good life, which included leisure, community interaction, and, yes, a particular convenience for members of a dominant religion. This latter convenience may not be of itself constitutionally permissible, but there is no reason the community cannot take notice of the fact that Sunday is the most opportune and customary day to choose for rest. Anyone who recalls blue laws doubtless remembers them in a mood of some inconvenience—they made shopping difficult on Sundays—but perhaps with some affection too: Sundays were also a less hectic day for everyone, and everyone's involvement was necessary to the attainment of that end. A patchwork of exceptions based on individual circumstances would, Frankfurter wrote, simply have "reintroduce[d] into Sunday the business tempos of the week," defeating the purpose of the law, which was "the creation of an atmosphere" in which individuals lived and which they had no inherent right to disrupt.[11] The religious heritage of blue laws was part of the traditions of a community, which could not regard itself as existing simply in the here and now.

For the lone dissenter, Justice William O. Douglas, "custom and habit" were irrelevant to the constitutional issue if not outright irrational. Instead of recognizing a political community, he saw the case as a contest between isolated individuals and their neighbors: "[I] do not see how a State can make protesting citizens refrain from doing innocent acts on Sunday because the doing of those acts offends sentiments of their Christian neighbors."[12] Protecting Christians from feeling offended was not the purpose of the statute; Frankfurter's atmosphere of repose was. Still, Douglas's dissent correctly spotted and dissected the individualist flaw in Warren's majority opinion, noting that if the goal was health and hygiene, the state could simply prescribe a single day of rest other than Sunday or otherwise limit working hours. For Douglas, custom was useful only as an instrument of proscription. *"[I]n the light of our society's religious history* [judgment] cannot be avoided by arguing that a hypothetical lawgiver could find nonreligious reasons for fixing Sunday as a day of rest. The effect of that history is, indeed, still with us."[13]

It is. The question is why the history is problematic. Morality and law are inseparable. Mark Pulliam has observed: "As reflected by President George Washington's 1796 *Farewell Address,* the founding generation believed there could be no law without morality, no morality without religion, and no legal order if individual rights were all that mattered."[14] The First Amendment's proscription against establishing a national religion does not prohibit any law with a religious motive, especially where a secular purpose coincides with it. The politics of obligation would be willing to interrogate customs like blue laws but inclined to defer to them on the grounds that the generations through which tradition accreted may, together, have been wiser than we are right now. Judicial engagement, by and large, would not.

This chapter does not aspire to offer a comprehensive review of all theories of judicial engagement. Its focus, rather, is those that are most antipolitical. These particularly include Randy Barnett's Presumption of Liberty; the normative understanding of law; attempts to import the Declaration of Independence into the Constitution; and, finally, theories of natural law that would make judges arbiters of the community's values. We shall conclude with John O. McGinnis's "duty of clarity," which charts a middle, though not unproblematic, course through this terrain.

THE PRESUMPTION OF LIBERTY

Barnett's constitutional theory is grounded in a specific concept of rationality that is inadequate to the goods of politics. His is a sterile, axiomatic reason that recognizes the "is" but never the "ought," unless the "ought" is to allow individuals to do as they wish when they wish. On this understanding, there is no community, only individuals. Barnett, employing an axiomatic "given-if-then" understanding of rationality to natural law—that is, given the nature of things, if we want to achieve this, then we must do that—but separating the question of natural rights from "natural law ethics," concludes: "[R]especting natural rights, not the calculation and aggregation of subjective preferences, promotes the common good. And the common good is viewed, not as a sum of preference satisfaction, but as the ability of *each person* to pursue happiness, peace, and prosperity while acting in close proximity to others."[15]

The dichotomy between individuals and the community does not withstand close scrutiny. Barnett presents the common good as either the individualist freedom of every isolated person—in which case "common" good is an odd locution for it—or as "a sum of preference satisfaction." He in essence denies there is anything "common" about the good we share except insofar as our preferences or liberties happen coincidentally to overlap. But thinkers like Aristotle, St. Thomas Aquinas and Edmund Burke—as well as the American Founders—have recognized that the community itself, the res publica, has existential status and a good of its own that is *not* merely an aggregation of personal preferences.

Barnett identifies natural rights as the solution to the problem of social order, except that the social is reduced to the empirical fact of living with others. The community has no ontological status except insofar as it describes what sounds very much like the Hobbesian frontier: individuals live together and have to figure out how to do so without hurting each other. Barnett frames natural rights as measures that best solve the problems of knowledge, scarcity, and interest. In other words, each of us knows only his or her local situation but must live with others whose knowledge differs; our use of scarce resources means our actions affect each other; and we are tempted to make partial laws based on self-interest.

This leaves no room for the politics of obligation or for *McGowan*'s understanding of the atmosphere of a community. How might such an analysis have treated *McGowan*? The range of natural rights Barnett not only regards as desirable but also imputes to the constitutional text is broad. Barnett among others regard the Fourteenth Amendment, which applies to the states, as a shield for economic liberty.[16] Thus the claim that the Court brushed aside in *McGowan*, which was that businesses forced to close on Sundays for arbitrary reasons were deprived of the equal protection of the laws, requires attention.

Barnett's Presumption of Liberty arises from his attempt to derive a principle of legitimacy in the absence of the possibility of popular consent, which he describes as operative only in conditions of unanimity. His question, following Aquinas, is why laws should "bind in conscience" if individuals have not directly consented to them. But while Barnett reiterates Aquinas's question, he does not pursue it to Aquinas's answer. Aquinas does distinguish between human and divine law, but the distinction is by no means libertarian. He repeatedly counterposes the common good to the private good of individuals. He says human law is derived from divine law. It may be unjust: "Nevertheless even a wicked law, in so far as it retains some appearance of law though being enacted by one who has the power to make law, is derived from the eternal law."[17]

Barnett concludes that "a law is just, and therefore binding in conscience, if its restrictions are (1) necessary to protect the rights of others and (2) proper insofar as they do not violate the preexisting rights of the persons on whom they are imposed." The latter requirement "dispenses" with the need for consent since a person need not consent if a law does not violate his rights. This assessment of the necessity and propriety of laws appears early in Barnett's analysis as an assertive judicial function: barring the possibility of unanimous consent, "every freedom-restricting law must be scrutinized to see if it is necessary to protect the rights of others without improperly violating the rights of those whose freedom is being restricted."[18]

Barnett sees this standard as a test of whether the Constitution should bind us in conscience, but also argues that the Founding generation shared the contours of that commitment, which they are said to have expressed in the Ninth Amendment's requirement that "[t]he enumeration in the constitution of certain rights shall not be construed to deny or disparage others retained by the people."[19] These "retained" rights are prepolitical liberty rights and are to be accorded no less status or protection, Barnett argues, than others that the Constitution specifically articulates. The Privileges and Immunities Clause, which appears in Article IV of the Constitution and applies to the states through the Fourteenth Amendment, embodies these rights, which are not susceptible of exhaustive enumeration. "[T]he classical conception of natural rights or liberties, as understood by the founders, could not be limited to a specific list and was, in this respect, unbounded."[20]

It is less clear that this was the original meaning of either the Ninth or Fourteenth Amendment. The Ninth, which was meant to address the fear that not all rights would be enumerated in a bill of rights, warns that "[t]he enumeration in the Constitution, of certain rights, shall not be construed to deny or disparage others retained by the people." As his critics are wont to note, Robert Bork famously or, depending on one's view, infamously compared the amendment to text covered by an inkblot whose meaning could not be ascertained. The metaphor would have been better put as an inkblot test: because the Ninth Amendment is too imprecise for judicial application, judges can see in it whatever they choose.

With respect to the rights protected by the amendment, everything hangs on the meaning of "others," which is different from saying "all" rights. Kurt T. Lash argues that the Ninth and Tenth Amendments should be read in tandem as a one-two punch maintaining the principle of enumerated powers while also protecting federalism. The Ninth, on his analysis, establishes a rule of strict construction. The Federalist concern about a bill of rights was not merely that it would not be exhaustive but also that it would alter the nature of a government of enumerated powers by denying it authorities it never had in the first place. The Ninth Amendment prevents the Bill of Rights from being "construed" to imply Congress had further powers than those enumerated in Article I, Section 8 of the Constitution. This coupling of the Ninth and Tenth Amendments is bolstered by the fact that Framers of the Fourteenth Amendment who understood its "privileges and immunities" to incorporate the Bill of Rights referred repeatedly only to the first *eight* amendments, not to the Ninth.[21]

Raoul Berger similarly observes that "the ninth deals with *rights* 'retained by the people,' the tenth with *powers* 'reserved' to the states or the people. As Madison perceived, they are two sides of the same coin." On this reading, the Ninth Amendment's original purpose was to leave rights in the hands of local government, not to nationalize new claims of freedom from the community's authority. Berger, like Lash, so understands Madison's original language, which said that "exceptions . . . made in favor of particular rights, shall *not* be construed to diminish the just importance of other rights retained by the people, or as to *enlarge the powers* delegated by the constitution." That is, as Berger notes, Madison explicitly disclaims any intent to enlarge national power by means of the Ninth Amendment. It is simply mirrors reflecting mirrors to incorporate, as many devotees of engagement would, the Ninth Amendment through the Fourteenth.[22] Larry D. Kramer writes that the guarantees of the Ninth Amendment were not open-ended. "The most logical reading of the Ninth Amendment's reference to 'other' rights 'retained by the people,' then, is to rights already or potentially secured within the customary constitutional tradition."[23]

As Wallace Mendelson has observed, the lack of "guiding standards or criteria" in the Ninth Amendment makes its rights "a nonjusticiable, political question."[24] In other words, assertions of Ninth Amendment rights belong in political forums like Congress, not the courts. In fact, the Fourteenth Amendment is emphatic on this point, empowering Congress and not the courts to enforce the amendment legislatively. There is nothing incongruous about rights being political questions, nor is it reading the Ninth Amendment out of the Constitution to say that they are. There are no *textual* grounds for proceeding to supply a rule like the Presumption of Liberty for the Ninth Amendment simply on the argument that it has to mean something, and something justiciable at that.

As to the Fourteenth Amendment, proponents of judicial engagement variously read it as imposing everything from John Stuart Mill's harm principle to the Bill of Rights to whatever judges ascertain would not have been part of a rational person's assent to a social compact. The result is what Richard M. Reinsch II, a critic, calls "natural rights nationalism" and what Barnett, a supporter, calls "Fundamental Rights Federalism."[25] Reinsch's label is more apt. With respect to these "fundamental rights," there is little left of federalism, as Barnett—who argues the Fourteenth Amendment was meant fundamentally to alter the mechanics of federalism in favor of national supervision of state laws where assertions of rights are involved—acknowledges.

There is an excellent historical case for reading the Bill of Rights into the Fourteenth Amendment's Privileges and Immunities Clause and an equally compelling jurisprudential argument that doing so would, in Mendelson's paraphrase of Justice Hugo Black, "anchor the generalities of the Fourteenth Amendment in the more 'clearly marked . . . boundaries' of the Bill of Rights," by which he meant the first eight, not the first nine, amendments.[26] On historical grounds, Berger would limit these further to the rights specified in the Civil Rights Act of 1866, which the Fourteenth Amendment was drafted to constitutionalize.[27] Beyond that, the Fourteenth Amendment becomes simply a grab bag of asserted rights on which there is no basis for reaching consensus or establishing limits.

On Barnett's understanding, by contrast, the amendments protect the liberties only of individuals, as opposed to, for example, rights of the community to establish a moral environment. Barnett denies that he "assume[s] 'atomistic' individuals. Rather, natural rights are those rights that are needed precisely to protect individuals and associations from the power of others—including the power of the stronger, of groups, and of the State—when and only when persons are deeply enmeshed in a social context."[28] This analysis wholly privatizes the classical understanding of politics. The claim of atomization is not that individuals do not know each other; it is that they cannot obligate each other except for the duty of each individual not to invade the isolated rights of every other.

The incompatibility of Barnett's analysis with the politics of obligation is evident in his use of originalism not as a theory of generational duty and promise-keeping but rather because it "is entailed by a commitment to a written constitution, which is a vital means of subjecting lawmakers to limits on their lawmaking powers."[29] Originalism, in other words, is instrumentally valuable for cabining government; it does not of itself make any normative demands. "[W]e are bound to respect the original meaning of a text, not by the dead hand of the past, but because we today—right here, right now—profess our commitment to this written Constitution, and original meaning interpretation follows naturally from this commitment."[30] Indeed, Barnett finds the "'dead hand' objection" to be the most potent one to originalism. "Why are we bound by the intentions, expectations, or original meanings of long-dead ancestors—in my case and most others, someone else's ancestors at that?" But the politics of obligation does not require direct descent from the *Mayflower* to impose itself. Those of us descended from far more recent immigrants need only regard ourselves as willingly adopted political descendants of these constitutional ancestors. "These" is important. Our ancestors did not join a mere axiom; they joined a political community with a particular and binding set of customs and understandings. Judges are neither authorized nor competent to legislate what those customs and understandings are. Bickel would take this further: "For many reasons that have no specific relation to the constitutional text, most of us treasure our nationhood, glory in much of our common past, and deeply want our posterity to live as we have done, in membership of this nation." The Constitution and Court are, for Bickel, mere symbols and sharpeners of "feelings that start by being shared, however nebulously."[31]

To be sure, he denies that judicial engagement authorizes judges to legislate custom. Barnett prefers the term "judicial nullification" to "judicial review" because of the corruption of the latter term to encompass commands to the political branches. "The confusion of judicial nullification with judicial supremacy arises if one ignores the proposition that judicial negation is not legislation." But negation—in the sense of declining to pass a bill, for example, including on constitutional grounds—is very much a legislative function, and there is a clear sense, Brutus's sense, in which allowing judges to pronounce last in sequence makes them supreme at least on constitutional questions: There is no appeal from their decisions except by the extraordinary mechanism of constitutional amendment. Barnett casts this instead as judicial equality, a term we have already seen is freighted with meanings with which neither the Founders nor the Court itself have imbued it.[32]

A standard is needed for the exercise of this purportedly coequal authority, partly in order to construe clauses of the Constitution that pertain to rights that are not enumerated. Consequently, rather than the traditional "presumption of constitutionality," according to which judges should uphold the constitutionality of laws barring overwhelming evidence to the contrary, Barnett would have judges operate on a sympathetic Presumption of Liberty that favors the citizen and requires the government to prove the necessity and propriety of enactments that restrict freedom. Liberty is "properly bounded freedom," which is to say freedom that does not encroach on the rights of others.[33]

Barnett supplies several illuminating examples of the Presumption of Liberty, of which we shall focus on two. One is the debate over a national bank in the First Congress, which Barnett uses to illustrate the belief among prominent Founders that the Necessary and Proper Clause required a serious degree of necessity, not just usefulness. We have already considered Madison's eloquent speech on this topic, in which he supplied rules of constitutional interpretation and construction, in chapter 3. For Barnett, the question of the power to incorporate the Bank was a question of constitutional construction, and Madison said that what became the Ninth Amendment, then under consideration by the states, "furnished" the rule. Yet it is significant that this discussion occurred far later in the speech than the reference to the "rule furnished by the constitution," as it had to since the amendments were not yet ratified and thus supplied no lawful standard. Even then, Madison described the Ninth (then Eleventh) Amendment as "guarding against a latitude of interpretation": in otherwise, not as a fount of unenumerated rights but rather as a guarantee that the enumerated powers would be construed strictly.

On Barnett's reading, the Necessary and Proper Clause needed a vigorous and narrow reading that restricted the national government to means for the enumerated powers that were truly necessary and proper. "[F]or Madison, whether or not a proposed action of government that restricted the liberty of the people was necessary, and therefore within the powers of Congress to enact, required some assessment of whether the means chosen were essential to the pursuit of an enumerated end." Even for John Marshall, who ruled on the issue in *McCulloch v. Maryland,* necessity required some showing, just not one that reached all the way to "indispensable necessity."

These are interesting debates that touch upon the most pressing constitutional questions, ones in which Barnett's middle path between Madison and Marshall is compelling. But there is also a sense in which this focus on the trees of constitutional dispute ignores the forest, which is the decisive fact that the most eloquent and searching debates on the constitutionality of the bank, from Hamilton's and Thomas Jefferson's dueling opinions for President Washington, to Madison's speech on interpretation and construction, occurred in the elected branches a full generation before they were litigated. Madison was instructing the legislative body on how to conduct its own work of constitutional interpretation. That speech was in 1791, and Marshall did not rule in *McCulloch* until 1819, twenty-eight years after the bank had so enmeshed itself into the national economy—indeed, after President Madison himself had acknowledged its constitutionality as having been established through generational consensus—that suddenly overturning it judicially was not a serious option.

Barnett infers judicial authority over the Necessary and Proper Clause from its use of the word "shall," which he correctly notes sounds like a command. The phrase does not give Congress "discretion over the application of the standard it supplies," discretion that would have triggered widespread opposition to the Constitution. "This strongly suggests that whatever meaning the clause had, it must be one that is justiciable."[34] The suggestion in question appears to arise from logic something like the following: Someone must police Congress's application of a constitutional standard, judges apply law, and therefore judges are the proper check. Judges may be *an* appropriate check, but especially against the broader backdrop of Madison's thought, nothing about this logic dictates the linear model of interpretation or construction according to which that check is the final constitutional word. After all, there are other actors in the constitutional system capable of checking Congress, from its own dissenting members to the president to the voters.

Speaking again to Congress, as Barnett notes, Madison denied that "necessary" meant "expedient" and proceeded to the question of judicial authority: "[W]e are told for our comfort that the judges will rectify our mistakes; how are the judges to determine in the case; are they to be guided in their decisions by the rules of expediency?" For Barnett, this argument does not reject judicial review, it rather rejects a standard of constitutionality that would preclude judicial review."[35] This is unclear. Even a stricter rule of necessity would involve judges in resolving questions of legislative discretion unless the term is meant—as indeed Jefferson appeared to understand it—to preclude Congressional action except where no alternative to the purportedly "necessary" action is available, a standard virtually impossible to meet.

Barnett suggests we look at the terms in reverse: "necessary" implies the possibility of "unnecessary," while "proper" indicates that there must be something that would make laws "improper." "[I]f the clause requires (a) a showing of means-ends fit—as per Madison, Jefferson, and even Hamilton—together with a showing that (b) the means chosen do not prohibit the rightful exercise of freedom (or violate principles of federalism or separation of powers) and (c) the claim by Congress to be pursuing an enumerated end is not a pretext for pursuing other ends not delegated to it (as per Marshall in *McCulloch*), then an inquiry into each of these issues is clearly within the competence of courts."[36] This requires further scrutiny.

The power to evaluate whether the means a legislature chooses fit a given end inherently involves some policy discretion. The question may be one of the degree of scrutiny. As Michael W. McConnell has noted, without some scrutiny, any policy can be validated by a chain of inferences. "But serious means-end scrutiny necessarily transfers essentially political judgments to the courts."[37] Alexander Hamilton does not seem to endorse such close scrutiny. "Means-end fit" requires, as the standard suggests, a link between necessary means and appropriate ends, such that Hamilton, the bank's champion, acknowledged that "[t]he relation between the measure and the end; between the nature of the mean employed toward the execution of a power, and the object of that power; must be the criterion of constitutionality; not the more or less of necessity or utility." But the sentence immediately preceding and contextualizing this in Hamilton's opinion states that "[t]he degree in which a measure is necessary, can never be a test of the legal right to adopt it; that must be a matter of opinion, and can only be a test of expediency." Just after that paragraph, he states a contrary principle of construction, which is that powers of government "ought to be construed liberally in advancement of the public good." Hamilton is unavailing here because he recognizes that the fit between means and ends is *both* a constitutional and a political judgment: that is, a constitutional judgment for the elected branches to make.

Madison and Jefferson, to whom Barnett attributes the view "that 'necessary' means that a given law must be incidental and closely connected to an enumerated power," are scarcely more help. Jefferson was a departmentalist who explicitly denied the authority of courts to declare laws unconstitutional outside the judiciary's sphere of operation. An understanding by which the judiciary pronounced authoritatively and last would make the Constitution, he wrote, "a complete *felo de se*."[38] Madison, like Marshall, noticed that the Necessary and Proper Clause enlarged rather than restricted congressional authority. As we have seen, in discussing *Cohens v. Virginia,* Madison said the Necessary and Proper Clause was "subjoined" to and thus widened Congress' authority over the capital district. "All that could be exacted however by these considerations would be, that the means of execution should be of the most obvious & essential kind."

Madison comes closest to endorsing judicial review of means-end fit in the Virginia Report of 1800, his effort to explain the Virginia legislature's 1798 resolutions opposing the Alien and Sedition Acts. Madison there criticizes the argument of supporters of the Sedition law that it was a "necessary and proper" adjunct of the power to punish insurrection: That is, if Congress could punish the crime, did it not have the power to punish acts that would induce it? Madison's argument bears extended quotation.

> This branch of the subject will be closed with a reflection which must have weight with all; but more especially with those who place peculiar reliance on the Judicial exposition of the constitution, as the bulwark provided against undue extensions of the Legislative power. If it be understood that the powers implied in the specified powers, have an immediate and appropriate relation to them, as means, necessary and proper for carrying them into execution, questions on the constitutionality of laws passed for this purpose, will be of a nature sufficiently precise and determinate for Judicial cognizance and controul. If, on the other hand, Congress are not limited in the choice of means by any such appropriate relation of them to the specified powers; but may employ all such means as they may deem fitted to *prevent* as well as to *punish*, crimes subjected to their authority; such as may have a *tendency* only to *promote* an object for which they are authorized to provide; every one must perceive that questions relating to means of this sort, must be questions of mere policy and expediency; on which legislative discretion alone can decide, and from which the judicial interposition and controul are completely excluded.[39]

There are Madisonian grounds here for judicial review of the Necessary and Proper Clause, and the passage underscores Barnett's argument that Madison does not mean to reject the mechanism but rather to find a justiciable standard for its exercise. But notice the circumstances: this was a case of criminal prosecutions and thus partook of what Madison, speaking in Philadelphia, called "a judiciary nature." It is significant that Madison did not, in his initial speeches, mention judicial supervision of the decision regarding a national bank. Earlier in the Virginia Report, Madison had warned against the claim that "the judicial authority is to be regarded as the sole expositor of the Constitution, in the last resort," partly on the ground that "there may be instances of usurped power, which the forms of the Constitution would never draw within the controul of the judicial department."[40]

The second component of Barnett's standard equates propriety variously with an enactment's compatibility with separation of powers, federalism and the background rights of others. Yet there is no evidence the Framers saw the role of the courts as policing separation of powers, which *Federalist* no. 51 says will be maintained by the natural attraction and repulsion of all three branches. The evidence for a final judicial say over questions of federalism is stronger but still mixed. What we must really face is the issue of the background rights of the people, which Barnett would protect on the basis of a Presumption of Liberty. But the Presumption of Liberty is fundamentally antipolitical, a characterization to which Barnett might not object. Its functional effect is inherently to inhibit the action of the community.

We might therefore profitably ask how it would apply, for example, to blue laws like the ones at stake in *McGowan*. Recall that "We the People" is a fiction for Barnett, so blue laws simply pit, in Hobbesian manner, the individuals resisting them against the apparently foreign legislators imposing them. Barnett would presumably recognize a liberty interest of each citizen to engage in commercial activity so long as doing so inflicts no wrong on others. But suppose the state replies that it *does* inflict a harm, not on discrete individuals—as in Douglas's claim that blue laws could not be sustained because they offended individual Christians—but rather on the atmosphere for repose the community wishes to facilitate? In this instance, to recur to Adam J. White's phrase, government is on trial. Its agents bear the burden of proof to show it is pursuing a necessary end by proper means. But if the means infringe a reserved right to economic activity, they are intrinsically improper.

As to the ends, *McGowan* is complicated by the fact that state rather than federal authority is being examined. For this we must look to Barnett's understanding of the Fourteenth Amendment has having nationalized the liberty interests of the people, and thus the second instance Barnett cites that merits scrutiny: the *Slaughter-House Cases*,[41] which produced an early and seminal Fourteenth Amendment ruling that Barnett argues improperly decimated the Privileges and Immunities Clause of that provision.

Taking his bearings from the dissents in the case, which dealt with a monopoly Louisiana established over slaughterhouses in New Orleans on grounds of public health, Barnett asserts that the Privileges and Immunities Clause of the Fourteenth Amendment "require[s] that legislation that purported to 'regulate' or modify the exercise of any civil right—including that to life, liberty, and property—be both necessary and proper for the common good," though he is comfortable "using the Due Process Clause to do the work of the Privileges and Immunities Clause [because] the due process of law includes judicial review."[42] Here Barnett makes a crucial turn in the direction of substantive due process: "[A] vital element of the 'due process of law' is the judicial scrutiny of the necessity and propriety of legislation. Allowing legislatures to deprive any person of life, liberty, or property without providing a judicial forum in which the limits of legislative power can be contested and adjudicated is a denial of this due process."[43] In other words, among the processes people are due is the right to challenge the constitutionality of laws in court, a standard that would to make all constitutional disputes judicial disputes. He consequently offers two stark choices: "Are all restrictions on the liberties of the people to be presumed constitutional unless an individual can convince a hierarchy of judges that the liberty is somehow 'fundamental?' Or should we presume that any restriction on the rightful exercise of liberty is unconstitutional unless and until the government convinces a hierarchy of judges that such restrictions are both necessary and proper?"[44]

This verges on argument by definition: judicial review is part of due process, and therefore due process is denied if judicial review is unavailable. Both options simply presume the sole or final authority of judges over constitutional disputes; that such issues should be matters of legislative debate or executive deliberation seems not to be a possibility, so the only question is which standard the "hierarchy of judges" should follow. The answer, crucially, is that the community bears the burden to convince judges not directly accountable to it that its intended acts are "necessary and proper." Judges must be assertive in this inquiry, seeking to smoke out—as the third component of Barnett's test above suggests—not just unnecessary means to improper ends but also presumably acceptable means that are actually, though not concededly, motivated by impermissible ends.

In the case of *Lochner v. New York*, long an object of criticism by proponents of judicial restraint and more recently one of revisionist rehabilitation,[45] Barnett notes the Court refused to accept the "mere assertion" of a statute's necessity and propriety.

> Thus, the doctrine of *Lochner*—and all the cases in which the court used the Due Process Clause of the Fourteenth Amendment to protect liberty—boils down to a proposition that some today find shocking: When the liberty of the individual clashes with the power of the state, the Court would not accept the "mere assertion" by a legislature that a statute was necessary and proper. Instead, it required a showing that a restriction of liberty have a "direct relation, as a means to an end," and that "the end itself must be appropriate and legitimate."[46]

As with Clark M. Neily III, there is no res publica mediating between the people and the state. There is a clash between them, with the legislature acting on the individual as a foreign object to which he or she bears no relation. As the epigraph to this chapter indicates, Barnett's legislature does not embody popular will or the common good because the legislators are merely a subset of the people chosen by a subset of the electorate. Moreover, the propriety and legitimacy of the end require the court to "review the rationality of such a judgment."[47] The *Lochner* Court thus took it upon itself to decide that limits on working hours did not affect the health of bakers or the quality of bread. This is a matter of legislative prudence transferred to the courts by means of the assumption that the Fourteenth Amendment, whose fifth section assigns Congress rather than the courts authority to enforce the amendment legislatively, confers on the federal judiciary the power to supervise state legislation.

Barnett proposes that the police power of states, which the Constitution never sets out to define, is a matter of construction because the Constitution does not specify it.[48] But on Barnett's own reading, the Constitution is not a comprehensive blueprint for all assertions of authority within its borders. It is a charter of national government imbued only with enumerated powers, so its silence on the residual authority of states does not open the door to construction. Nevertheless, in Barnett's treatment, the police power becomes the power to protect "individual rights" and as such is subject to the Presumption of Liberty: "The Presumption of Liberty places the burden of establishing the propriety of laws on the government. The government may meet its burden by showing that any restrictions on individuals are either prohibitions on wrongful conduct or proper regulations of rightful activity."[49]

By this, he means the activity of isolated individuals. Blue laws clearly do not meet the former test, since Barnett's understanding of "wrongful" is individual conduct that harms another person. Nor could they meet Barnett's test of propriety. The Presumption of Liberty would more or less read Mill's harm principle into the Constitution, which would, incidentally, have made the Constitution, and especially its Fourteenth Amendment, a much shorter and simpler document.[50] Barnett writes: "[G]overnment could not use its unenumerated police power to prohibit the possession or use of any object that, if properly used, does not pose an unreasonable risk of violating the rights of others."[51] Since the "others" are "individuals," there is no room in this understanding for a community to have rights, such as to preserve a way of life that requires a certain environment in which individuals can exert their political natures. There are only individuals being oppressed by legislators who are themselves mere individuals.

Moreover, the requirement that legislation be "rational" is a burden many laws will be unable to meet if rationality excludes considerations of traditional or moral values.[52] Recall that this always means what can be axiomatically demonstrated to be rational right now, not what generations have regarded as wise or prudent. The aggregated wisdom of the ages, which is not always evident in the moment, cannot pass this test, at least with any consistency. If rationality requires axiomatic proof, then doing something because it is customary is unlikely to be upheld as a "rational" basis for legislation. Yet it bears emphasis that Justice Anthony Kennedy's jurisprudence of "dignity," which has been responsible for such cases as *Lawrence v. Texas*, is shot through with moral argumentation.[53]

Indeed, we can push the point further. As Frankfurter suggested, few laws have single purposes. Barnett quotes Justice Clarence Thomas ruling in a 1993 case that "we never require a legislature to articulate its reasons for enacting a statute," so any conceivable purpose suffices to pass constitutional muster. Yet a legislature can rarely articulate a discrete purpose to legislation, because legislation is the product of many minds making many compromises in response to many pressures. Politics is a messy business, and it is within neither the authority nor the capacity of judges to tidy it.

EPSTEIN'S ECONOMIC CONSTITUTIONALISM

Richard Epstein offers one of the most subtle accounts of judicial assertiveness, acknowledging frankly, as has been seen above, that the original Constitution does not provide for judicial supremacy but that prescription—the law of long usage—does. Yet the standards Epstein would apply for judicial analysis substantially exceed even the most generous reading of settled practice. Epstein offers a perceptive economic analysis of the Takings Clause, including regulatory takings under which private property may be taken only under three conditions: it must be justified "to protect against wrongs that the property owner committed against others"; for a genuinely public use or by the owner's consent; and, finally, with just compensation.[54]

Epstein is unquestionably right about the sanctity of property to the Framers and to ongoing liberty and economic health, even if a full discussion of the question of regulatory takings exceeds the scope of this study. His reach is in the attempt to apply the same framework to "all constitutional cases of individual rights." The "public use" provision of his framework—which would, by analogy, suggest that liberties could be restricted for a public purpose—seems to disappear at this juncture of his analysis. Instead, we are left with what amounts to constitutionalizing the harm principle. Consider this passage: "Similarly, the state can enjoin the operation of a public nuisance, but it cannot simply designate so-called adult theaters as nuisances that can be shut down by the state. Nor can the state treat other activities like flag-burning or private sexual conduct as nuisances, even when others rightly find them offensive or unpatriotic."[55] Why, exactly, can adult theaters not be treated as nuisances? Apparently because they do not entail *individuals* harming *individuals.* Society as an ontological concept is nowhere to be found. Epstein specifically denies such a concept: "[P]ropositions about 'public,' 'society,' or 'the community' are not statements about organic groups that have value independent of the individuals who compose them. To the contrary, claims about the benefits and harms to society have to be broken down into statements about the benefits and harms to real people."[56] Epstein does, in fairness, acknowledge that the boundaries of a right must be set before this degree of protection begins. But the boundaries appear to be established by the harm principle. He would take this point, apparently, to the extremity of the Constitution "militat[ing] strongly to a flat tax,"[57] a supremely prudential question.

BEGGING THE QUESTION OF LAW

For many if not most proponents of judicial engagement, "law" does not merely mean a rule promulgated in advance in known fashion. They read "law" normatively *and* would empower judges to supervise that question. Barnett, for example, quotes Aquinas to the effect that "only just laws 'have the power of binding in conscience,'" which "informs [Aquinas's] endorsement of Augustine's statement that 'that which is not just seems to be no law at all'; therefore the *force* of a law depends on the extent of its justice." This may be true of the moral force of law—though even there Aquinas says it is possible there would be an obligation to obey to avoid "scandal or disturbance"[58]—but the Thomist treatment is more nuanced. Aquinas earlier says that "law must attend to the ordering of individual things in such a way as to secure common happiness."[59] This "common happiness" has ontological status and pertains not to hedonistic but rather to virtuous ends. Moreover, he does not release the individual from a practical obligation of obedience on the grounds of a law's asserted injustice.[60]

Timothy Sandefur also packs into the word "law" all the normative meanings he proceeds to extract from it. Emphasizing that the Fifth and Fourteenth Amendments require not just "due process" but also due process "*of law*," Sandefur contrasts law with arbitrariness, a term he acknowledges is imprecise. But "we can say that an arbitrary act is an act that does not accord with any rational rule or explanatory principle, an act that has no connection to a larger purpose or goal."[61] This, he explains, suggests a teleological understanding of government. A law is not law simply because an authority says it is but rather because of its "underlying logic or correspondence to principle." Sandefur notes that a policy choice does not violate that standard simply by virtue of imprecision: There are, he observes, several ages at which a young person might be said to reach the age of maturity, and any choice in that range is permissible "[s]o long as each alternative is within the realm of reasonable choices."[62] In a case of law, the legislating authority should be able to give a reason as to why it did one thing and not another. "Because we wanted to," in other words, is arbitrary and not lawful, as are rules meant to advantage the ruler rather than the ruled.

Sandefur argues that a rule can be lawless for violating "implicit or inherent limits on government power." The state's lawful authority is to be ascertained by reference to "the purposes for which the state was formed," such that acts that cannot be so justified are not laws and therefore violate the Due Process Clause. What, then, are the purposes of American government? "Classical liberals like the Framers envisioned government not only as an arbitrator but also as analogous to a security guard."[63] Sandefur approvingly cites Justice Samuel Chase's claim in *Calder v. Bull* that the Constitution should be interpreted according to "[t]he purposes for which men enter into society,"[64] though how Sandefur would account for Chase's highly partisan support of the Sedition Act is unclear unless he means to confess the fallibility of judges, which would admit the Paradox of Engagement. The purposes for which the Constitution was formed, Sandefur says, are stated in its preamble, the only provision of which he cites, significantly, is its reference to "secur[ing] the blessings of liberty."

We are running in circles here. It is difficult to distinguish Sandefur's normative understanding of law from Ronald Dworkin's "Moral Reading of the Constitution," which would give judges an extraordinary warrant to police the justice of laws based on "abstract moral principle[s]."[65] McConnell notices that "[i]t is easy to see why these arguments would appeal to law professors, who share with federal judges a common background, social class, and education," but concludes that while "[w]e have heard a lot about 'principle' and 'the correct standard' and 'integrity,' I think we need to hear more about judicial humility. All of the various constraints on judicial discretion can be understood as means of tempering judicial arrogance by forcing judges to confront, and take into account, the opinions of others."[66] There is some irony in judicial engagement's combination of an antipolitical, antimajoritarian perspective with a normative reading of law, since the law must, after all, come from somewhere. Given the breadth of purposes of the Constitution—which, we should bear in mind, was a response to the impotence of the Articles of Confederation regime and thus aimed to establish adequate power at the center—Sandefur has erected a standard according to which judges determine what suits such purposes as "the general welfare," "the common defense," and so forth.

Moreover, Sandefur gives short shrift to Justice James Iredell's famous concurrence in *Calder*, in which he argued that the Supreme Court could exercise the "delicate and awful" power of judicial nullification only in "a clear and urgent case." Iredell continued: if a legislature passes a law pursuant to a constitutional authority, "the Court cannot pronounce it to be void, merely because it is, in their judgment, contrary to the principles of natural justice. The ideas of natural justice are regulated by no fixed standard: the ablest and the purest men have differed upon the subject," such that all judges could do in such a situation was comment that they believed the law in question violated "the abstract principles of natural justice."[67] Sandefur allows that Iredell's view is "certainly understandable" since judges could "exploit their power to interpret the Constitution's implicit principles to nullify laws they simply dislike." However, he concludes, this is "a prudential, not a legal argument."[68] It is neither. It is a political argument, grounded in the realities of how people with power behave. One can hope for prudential judges, but since enlightened jurists will not always be at the helm, one must plan otherwise. Iredell's meaning is not that natural justice does not exist, but rather than it lacks the outward and definitive signs that enable judges to apply it with precision and objectivity. This is not merely prudential. It is an argument about the nature of this conception of justice and its inherent propensity for abuse.

The question is one of authority—not whether decisions should be based on natural justice, but rather *whose* decisions, elected officials' or judges', should be so grounded. Sandefur confuses *The Federalist*'s teaching on this, arguing that the Constitution constrained government to its purposes through democracy, the Bill of Rights, and "creat[ing], within limits, 'a will in the community independent of the majority'"; that is, the judiciary. This last reference is to *Federalist* no. 51, which explicitly *rejects* creating a will independent of the majority, instead favoring the multiplicity and diversity of interests that Madison believed would address the problem of majority abuse without resorting to institutional controls, including the courts. Significantly, Madison anticipates the Paradox of Engagement: an independent will—in Sandefur's view, the courts—"at best, is but a precarious security; because a power independent of the society may as well espouse the unjust views of the major, as the rightful interests of the minor party, and may possibly be turned against both parties." In other words, there is no reason to assume a will independent of the community would be any more of a safeguard for rights than republican institutions, and it might become hostile to liberty outright.

Yet consider the breadth of power Sandefur would give to judges:

> If a court is called upon to determine whether a challenged statute is
> lawful or arbitrary, then the court must be prepared to look behind
> the statute's form and examine its substance. It must determine
> whether the principle the ruler purports to be advancing in its
> legislation is genuine or only illusory. This means that it is not
> in principle possible for courts to avoid addressing the question
> of whether a challenged law advances a legitimate government
> interest—or deciding which government interests are or are not
> "legitimate." These are inherently normative questions, but as long
> as judges are in the business of determining *what* the law is, they
> will be called upon to make value-laden determinations of what is
> a general principle of lawfulness and what is merely an arbitrary
> assertion of power. To put this in modern parlance: So long as
> courts must decide whether a law is rationally related to a legitimate
> government interest, they cannot hope to avoid determining what is
> and is not a legitimate government interest. "Is" and "ought" cling
> together in this undertaking.[69]

Several problems proceed from this analysis. One is that on a normative concept of law—"telocratic" rather than "nomocratic," to use
Michael Oakeshott's dichotomy[70]—judges cannot escape prudential decisions about what rules are and are not within a judicially determined
range of options, *without clear text to guide the courts' analysis.* Sandefur
does not mean merely that establishing a national religion exceeds that
range, on which everyone agrees—and the most potent barrier against
which, it bears mentioning, *Federalist* no. 51 says is not the courts but
rather the vast number of religious sects, which would prevent any one
from becoming a majority. Sandefur means that laws that jurists do not
believe relate rationally to a legitimate purpose of government as they
conceive it are subject to judicial review. The lines between legislative
and judicial authority inevitably blur into combination. As guardians of
the purposes of government and therefore the range of options available

to it, judges would exert extraordinary authority over policy that seems legislative in character.

In fact, it is difficult to see why Sandefur would allow the legislature much of a range at all. Speed limits, for example, vary substantially from state to state. Confining a driver to, say, sixty-five miles per hour when another state allows eighty restricts his or her liberty in a way that, on Sandefur's reasoning, seems judicially cognizable. The end—public safety—is legitimate, but are the "means" arbitrary? Suppose evidence from states where the speed limit is higher indicates that eighty miles per hour is as safe as sixty-five. It appears that a driver has a right to present such evidence to a judge to review whether the choice of sixty-five was arbitrary.

This is not to deny that "law" is a normative concept, as in Augustine's dictum that unjust laws seem not to be laws at all or Aquinas's that they partake more of "violence" because they bind through force rather than conscience. But Sandefur is importing the normative understanding of law into constitutional phrases meant to accomplish something else entirely: to ensure life, liberty, and property can be invaded only on the basis of known rules and fair procedures. There is no evidence that the Constitution empowers *judges* to assess the normative content of law. There is ample difference between saying laws should be assessed normatively and that judges should do the assessing. Allocating this authority to judges is an entirely different proposition from saying law should be ordered to justice.

The question is one of authority. Such arguments can and ought to be made to legislatures making laws. One of their most famous invocations was Martin Luther King Jr.'s "Letter from Birmingham Jail," which quoted Augustine's statement about unjust laws at the same time its author urged practitioners of nonviolence to accept the law's judgments and, indeed, even as he willingly submitted to a jail sentence for violating a law he believed was unjust. Arguments about the normative status of law can be powerful persuasive tools, but allowing judges to treat law normatively makes them censors over every decision of the community without any objectively known and agreed-upon standard to which they and the community can repair.

A second problem is that even if we accepted Sandefur's account of judicial power in its narrowest sense, we would still be left with the Paradox of Engagement: namely, trusting judges—who (a) are human and (b) wield power—to confine themselves to those narrow boundaries voluntarily. Yet a significant premise of judicial engagement in the first place is the propensity of power to be abused, a human condition to which there is no exemption for judges. Neither law school commencements nor judicial commissions entail a journey into the earth so Platonic gold can be poured into the anointed's soul.

We know judges make mistakes because, among other reasons, advocates of judicial engagement so often complain that they do. They routinely refer to a litany of judicial infamies, including *Buck v. Bell,* the forced-sterilization case, but the self-selective bias in filling the catalog of judicial outrage is remarkable. *Buck* was accomplished, to be sure, on wrong-headed assertions of judicial restraint, and Evan Bernick's ideal judge would have engaged instead. But what about a black robe makes it any likelier that a judge would use that philosophy to do right rather than wrong? The same is true of Congress's authority, of course, or the president's, but their errors are correctable at the ballot box. If anything, the extraordinary power judicial engagement would accord judges would be more temptation than trust. For every moment of moral exaltation the judiciary has provided, there are counterexamples of moral turpitude. *Brown v. Board of Education* was necessary because the Court erred in *Plessy v. Ferguson.* One of its earliest substantive due process cases was *Dred Scott v. Sandford,* in which Chief Justice Roger Taney explicitly employed that framework to invalidate the Missouri Compromise.

To be sure, he applied it wrongly. The question for judicial engagement is why, generally speaking, we should trust judges any more than legislators—whose civil rights record, Louis Fisher has shown,[71] is on the whole better than the judiciary's—to reach the right answer. Yet Sandefur shows an astonishing degree of faith in the very lawyers whom he pillories in other contexts: "Aside from cynical prejudice," writes Sandefur, whose distrust of government is rooted in cynicism, "there is no reason to think that people generally read the Constitution to endorse their preferred policy outcomes. Moreover, people are typically drawn to study the Constitution in the first place because they approve, at least in general, of the Constitution as they understand it." True, lawyers are trained in questions of justice, but so are philosophers and political theorists. There is no particular reason to believe the detached reason of any of these experts would be superior to the deliberation of a republican people.

The normative concept of law, for Sandefur as for Arkes, often descends into what might be called the *reductio ad constitutionem*: the claim that a principle must be unconstitutional if it would lead to absurd or immoral results. In this mode of analysis, which disregards Burke's prudent dictum against reasoning from the extreme case, dystopian visions reign. Witness Sandefur's use of Shirley Jackson's story "The Lottery," in which the citizens of a town gather annually and choose a citizen at random to stone to death. Sandefur oddly says Tessie Hutchinson, the victim in the story, has been accorded "due process"—after all, the rules of the lottery were fair and known in advance—but not "of law," since no practice that takes life so arbitrarily could be called a "law."

Sandefur is swinging at a straw man; no one claims promulgation alone satisfies the due process of law. Hutchinson is given no process, much less "due" process. She is neither accused of nor tried for a crime. The more significant problem is that the example's use of a corrupt tradition misdiagnoses the illness: the regime in the story is sick to its core. Sandefur's illustration recalls Learned Hand's admonition "that a society so riven that the spirit of moderation is gone, no court *can* save; that a society where that spirit flourishes, no court *need* save; that in a society which evades its responsibility by thrusting upon the courts the nurture of that spirit, that spirit in the end will perish."[72] A regime so corrosive would easily dissolve what Madison derided as "parchment barriers," mere written constitutional commands there was no will to follow. Constitutions do not save societies that sick, and societies that corrupt do not abide by constitutions. What is perhaps most important is that, outside of dystopian fiction, regimes of this type tend not to last, which is another reason for deferring to the wisdom of enduring tradition. Sandefur's reliance on illustrations in extremis recalls Madison's admonition in *Federalist* no. 55 about the fevered scenarios of abuse conjured by Anti-Federalists:

> The sincere friends of liberty, who give themselves up to the extravagancies of this passion, are not aware of the injury they do their own cause. As there is a degree of depravity in mankind, which requires a certain degree of circumspection and distrust: so there are other qualities in human nature, which justify a certain portion of esteem and confidence. Republican government presupposes the existence of these qualities in a higher degree than any other form. Were the pictures which have been drawn by the political jealousy of some among us, faithful likenesses of the human character, the inference would be, that there is not sufficient virtue among men for self-government; and that nothing less than the chains of despotism can restrain them from destroying and devouring one another.[73]

Sandefur's criterion of legality—that a law must show "generality and public-orientation elements" to assure it is not "only an arbitrary assertion of force by those with greater political influence"—leaves little room for the community to act on values as a community rather than as a collection of individuals. It is suffused with what social scientists call "methodological individualism." To be sure, there is no constitutional warrant for these criteria in the first place—the Constitution rather says quite explicitly where government may not act; it does not incorporate Mill's harm principle—but the logic is worth following. Consider Sandefur's illustration for this point, *Lawrence v. Texas*, which created a constitutional right to same-sex intimacy. For Sandefur, a ban on homosexual sodomy is unlawful because it "did not realistically advance any genuine public good,"[74] on which grounds judges rather than legislators determine how "genuine" a public good is. One need not endorse such bans—I for the record do not—to see that if society is a mere collection of individuals and if private conduct is inherently unregulable, legislation whose aim is the fostering of a moral environment cannot survive.

Justice Scalia saw this in *Lawrence,* writing in dissent that it "effectively decrees the end of all morals legislation."[75] Bork called this phenomenon "the privatization of morality."[76] Yet morals legislation, while it may err, *is* publicly oriented and can be understood to serve general ends. The ultimate question is who is to decide which public ends are "genuine," which are not, and when the legislature is not just pursuing legitimate ends with permissible means but also doing so for sincere reasons.

Of course, as we have already seen, a legislature rarely speaks with one voice, which is one reason legislatures are so valuable. One answer to the problem to which many proponents of judicial engagement subscribe is that a judge must "scrutinize," to use Barnett's word, a law to ascertain its true motives. For example, Barnett, tracing morals legislation to the Progressive movement, says courts reacted to such laws by "realistically assess[ing] whether restrictions on liberty were truly calculated to protect the health and safety of the general public, rather than being the product of 'other motives' beyond the just powers of a republican legislature."[77] Barnett would have judges invalidate laws motivated by "(a) the desire to assist favored persons or groups at the expense of other citizens, (b) the desire to harm other individuals or groups, or (c) the desire to stigmatize or make more costly the exercise of a liberty of which some disapprove. In the absence of express consent, no citizen can be presumed to have consented to a lawmaking power with any of these as its purpose."[78] This sounds benign enough, except that, to consider just the first category, a very great deal of legislation, from the Tariff of 1828 to progressive taxation to Medicare and Medicaid, assists some people at the expense of others. Sandefur's claim that the Constitution was intended to inhibit government interference with the economy would have surprised Alexander Hamilton, the author of the *Report on Manufactures* and the champion of the First National Bank.

Barnett's standard would not prohibit such legislation, to be sure, at least not necessarily. The inquiry he seeks is in some ways more problematic: the question is not whether the legislation *does* these things but whether it was motivated by a *desire* to do these things. Thus one assumes that a desire to help the elderly with medical care might justify

Medicare even if it has the incidental effect of imposing a cost on other citizens. But this inquiry into motives, even if one assumes they exist in any discrete and identifiable form, treads deeply onto legislative terrain on what cannot help but be subjective grounds. It can also be easily circumvented by a legislature simply declaring a permissible purpose, which would require the judge, in turn, to weigh its sincerity.

Furthermore, to have judges inquire, as Neily would, into not just whether Congress considered constitutional issues but also *how* seriously it did so ignores the realities of legislative behavior, much of which consists of closed-door negotiations that produce no public record and almost none of which produces discrete reasons. Congress may debate the Constitution, may append constitutional findings to a bill, and still be vulnerable to a judicial finding—one to which one suspects judges, jealous for their own authority, would be innately tempted—to say Congress did not take the constitutional issues seriously enough, considered the wrong ones, or reached the wrong conclusion.

For Barnett, "[r]equiring the government to identify its true purpose and then show that the means chosen are actually well suited to advance that purpose helps smoke out illicit motives that the government is never presumed by a sovereign people to have authorized."[79] Yet this categorical statement that some things are unconstitutional not because the Constitution explicitly proscribes them but rather because a sovereign people, by which Barnett means sovereign individuals, would never authorize them is exceptionally subjective. There is nothing a judge could not sweep into the range of judicial authority if he or she is the supreme arbiter not of a written Constitution with specific authorizations and proscriptions but rather of that to which sovereign, and one presumes "rational," people would consent.

We have a process through which a sovereign people register their consent: elections.[80] We had one through which they indicated their assent to common goals and rules: constitutional ratification. Barnett denies that individual rights can be vindicated through the process of election because the individuals involved are often powerless and the issues in conflict obscure. Hence, "[o]nly by empowering the individual to bring suit before an impartial judiciary that will require government regulators to justify their restrictions on liberty as actually rational can these rights be vindicated in practice."[81]

This is a strange variety of originalism. It amounts to saying that because American government is larger and more complicated, which it was not at its origins, new methods of constitutional restraint, which were not prescribed at its origins, are necessary. The approach sounds close to two theories advocates of judicial restraint otherwise repudiate. The first is living constitutionalism, according to which judges must reinterpret the Constitution to keep up with modern realities its Framers could not anticipate. Advocates of judicial engagement would deny this: as originalists, they want the law interpreted according to its original meaning. What they are redefining is the authority of the judge who is doing the interpreting, and therein lies the irony: judicial engagement—which argues against allowing legislatures to judge their own authority—would have the jurist redefine his or her own authority.

The second theory that makes strange bedfellows of judicial engagement is the Progressive movement's ambition for "scientific legislation" based on identifiable goals and objective evidence. Woodrow Wilson, for example, complained that legislation had "little coherency" and that there was thus "little coherency about the debates."[82] Wilson's search for rationality led him to the presidency as a unifying and centralizing institution; judicial engagement has simply led it to judges instead. In either case it is a technocracy; the only question is whether the technocrats wear black robes or business suits.

Barnett, critiquing *Williamson v. Lee Optical Co.*, a case that chapter 5 will treat more fully, writes: "Traditionally, a law that was not 'logically consistent with its aims' was literally irrational and therefore unconstitutional." There is a leap here—an alluring one, to be sure, for no one likes laws that are logically inconsistent—and it is contained in the word "therefore." Barnett defines the irrational as unconstitutional. Irrational laws are, to put the matter succinctly, bad. Legislatures should not pass them and voters should advocate their repeal. But irrational and unconstitutional are distinct things, to say nothing of the fact that "unconstitutional" and "justiciable" differ too. To conflate all this is to make judges the superintendents of not merely the constitutionality but also the coherence and perhaps the wisdom or unwisdom of statutes. Again, much legislation that is the product of many minds, and especially of generational minds encoded in custom, cannot survive this inquiry.

To say, "Our community will do thus-and-such because our ancestors have done so and we wish our descendants to follow them" is a reason for a law, but one vulnerable to challenge by those who believe such reasoning to violate canons of rationality in the present. Consider one of the lower-court challenges to prohibitions on same-sex marriage. In *Kitchen v. Herbert,* US District Judge Robert J. Shelby struck down the state's prohibition on same-sex marriage, brushing aside arguments about what marriage had traditionally meant with the bromide, "tradition alone cannot form a rational basis for a law."[83] Regardless of one's prudential views on same-sex marriage, this opposition between tradition and rationality radically misses the point that the former is the storehouse and proving ground of the latter.

Barnett's proposal to replace the Presumption of Constitutionality with a Presumption of Liberty sounds different, and is constitutionally different, when an individual is pitted against the state than when political majorities confront political minorities. Barnett takes this as far as placing a burden on the government to justify a postal monopoly.[84] On Barnett's antipolitical account, the Constitution makes individuals, never the community, sovereign, and "[t]he 'due process of law' affords each person the opportunity to contest a deprivation of his or her life, liberty, or property as irrational or arbitrary before an independent tribunal of justice." This authority—recalling that constitutional questions on this view are always judicial ones—derives from the fact that the legislative power is limited not simply by the text of the Constitution but rather by the fact that "no rational person can be presumed to have consented to their liberty being irrationally or arbitrarily restricted."[85] This standard would thus be more precisely rendered as "no rational person would consent to what a judge calls irrational or arbitrary."

To be sure, rationality on Barnett's account is not entirely subjective. We have already seen that he would have judges review laws to ensure a means-end fit: that is, whether the government has utilized rational means to achieve a permissible end. The ends are limited, on his philosophical account, by the fact that individuals would not consent to irrational or arbitrary restrictions on their liberty. But this is hardly self-evident. It would be entirely rational for an individual to make a Madisonian bargain with three components. First, the individual agrees that he or she does not have all the information necessary for the just resolution of all questions, and would rather that such decisions in either case be made by elected officials from whom he or she has some recourse than by judges who are all but untouchable. Second, the individual accepts an obligation to his or her ancestors and descendants that may entail suppressing current preferences. Third, and crucially, the individual recognizes that he or she is a member of a political *community*. As such, his or her notion of justice will prevail on some issues and fall short on others, and he or she will accept the authority of the res publica either way. This last criterion is the essence of a Madisonian politics of shifting factions in which a loser one day accepts his fate because he can look forward to winning the next. For Barnett, there is neither a temporal nor a political perspective, only whether the individual or the state is entitled to win immediately.

It is equally important that Barnett repeatedly assumes, in a conclusion that contains its premise, that it is judges who are to make such decisions. Why not urge those with constitutional objections to present them to elected officials? That would involve the people in the healthy enterprise of constitutional conversation. They might well be discouraged from the hard work of doing so by the convenient ability to outsource the work to judges. Certainly it is the case that Congress and the president have so outsourced their constitutional oaths, enacting what they deem expedient on the grounds that the courts will stop them if they overreach. This seems consistent with judicial engagement's linear approach to constitutional interpretation, but it is incompatible with the Constitution's architecture for preventing abuse, which centers around the multidirectional controls of the separation of powers.

Barnett does not go that far, but his role for judges as overseers of the community's rationality or irrationality finds no basis in the Founding. It is also dangerous. Brutus reminds us to ask how a judge with such broad and unchallenged authority is likely to behave. White has posed the thought experiment of whether a proponent of judicial engagement would support a Supreme Court of one if he or she could pick the justice.[86] The reason we have nine is the need for deliberation and the possibility of error: because, in short, many constitutional questions do not have answers obviously derivable from clear axioms. Alexander Bickel observes: "[T]here are no ineluctable, universal, timeless absolutes in the art of ordering society; hence, as I remarked before, the most fundamental of one man's fundamental presuppositions, most ideally arrived at, will not always be another's. That is why we prefer a nine-man Court." Steven G. Calabresi, no advocate of judicial restraint, notes this need for deliberation and says the Court is better suited than Congress for it in constitutional matters.[87] But not from the perspective of accountability. Even the nine justices compose a small group that differs fundamentally from a sizable legislature deliberating at a step of remove from large populations. George W. Carey has observed that when imbued with the actuality or equivalent of policymaking authority, the justices strongly resemble the direct democracy Madison so feared in *Federalist* no. 10.[88] They are making policy, making it immediately, and making it in a perilously small group whose authority is binding. The conditions are ripe not for controlling factions—a role *The Federalist* never assigned the judiciary in the first place—but rather for acting like one.

THE DECLARATION AS JUDICIAL INSTRUMENT

Sandefur advances the case for judicial engagement by arguing that the Declaration of Independence frames—is "the conscience of"—the Constitution, such that "it is part of our fundamental law" and constitutional provisions should be interpreted in light of it.[89] He calls this an examination of "what Supreme Court Justice Benjamin Cardozo called 'our system of ordered liberty.' That system saw the relationship between order and liberty in a particular way: liberty comes first, and order arises from it."[90] That is manifestly not how Cardozo saw that "system": in *Palko v. Connecticut,* the case Sandefur quotes, Cardozo used "order" to limit, not to license, liberty, denying that the Fifth Amendment's protection against double jeopardy applied to the states because it was *not* "of the very essence of a scheme of ordered liberty." For Cardozo, only those liberties without which "a fair and enlightened system of justice would be impossible" should be judicially enforced against the states.[91]

For Sandefur, the Declaration of Independence "sets the framework for reading our fundamental law." The declaration is "a legal document—a part of the nation's organic law and the inspiration for America's Constitution. The declaration helps make constitutional priorities clear—that rights come first and government power only second—and thus it anchors our legal and political system on a firm philosophical ground." This "rights first, government second" paradigm flips Madison's, which Sandefur later quotes: "[Y]ou must first enable the government to control the governed; and in the next place oblige it to control itself." The more basic problem is Sandefur's mere assertion that the declaration forms the framework for the Constitution. If it did, and if, as Sandefur says, it creates a single people, those who immediately framed the Articles of Confederation must not have read the declaration before signing it. The Articles of Confederation contain nothing about rights and confer virtually all power on the states as political units. That is not to defend the articles, which were unworkable from their inception. It is, rather, to observe that those who framed both the declaration and the articles either did not understand the former or must not have shared Sandefur's conclusion that it was the fundamental law of the nation.

Obviously the declaration occupies a unique pride of place as the nation's first founding document. But it was a *legal* document—a law—only with respect to the act of separation it proclaimed. It was not the beginning of American ideas about politics, which had been germinating and evolving on this side of the Atlantic since the Mayflower Compact, decades before Locke.[92] It should guide our philosophical understanding

of our national purposes, but that makes it—or should—a tool for political debate. Its philosophical premises are not precise enough, nor is
there a scintilla of evidence they were intended, for judicial application.
Sandefur denies that the Founders were committed to democracy, a
word he notes appears neither in the Declaration of Independence nor
the Constitution. Yet "republican" does appear in the Constitution, in
one of the few provisions authorizing the national government to interfere with the states. It appears repeatedly in *The Federalist*. Nonetheless,
Sandefur avers:

> On the contrary, the Founders had different priorities. In the very
> first sentence of the Constitution, they pronounced unambiguously
> that liberty is a "blessing." They did not say the same about
> democracy. The Constitution they wrote imposes manifold limits
> on the power of the majority, some quite severe. . . . The Framers
> saw majority rule as a useful but dangerous device, to be deployed
> sparingly in order to protect freedom.[93]

The preamble does of course call liberty a blessing, or rather says it
is the "blessings" of liberty it aims to capture, perhaps as opposed to its
less sanguine dimensions.[94] That is the last in a serial listing of purposes,
and to quote it and not the others—such as "insur[ing] domestic Tran-
quility" and "promot[ing] the general Welfare," purposes that require
authority, not just the protection from it—deeply distorts the preamble. Perhaps more than any other advocate of judicial engagement, Sandefur would encode Mill in the Constitution: "[T]he Declaration . . .
describe[s] human rights as including 'life, liberty, and the pursuit of
happiness'—that is, an *indefinite* range of freedom, rather than a list of
specific liberties. Liberty does not come in discrete quanta; it is a general
absence of interference."[95] He would thus resist reducing the Constitution to a "bullet-point" document.

This is problematic on several counts. It is a standard method of interpretation to assume the Constitution used words parsimoniously, but the
document evidently wasted a great deal of them by not simply import-

ing the declaration's tripartite rights. Sandefur rejects this longstanding method of avoiding interpretations that lead to surplus language, replying glibly that lawyers are known to repeat themselves. Laying to one side the fact that the Constitution was neither framed nor ratified by lawyers alone, this rejection of standard interpretive method is necessary because Sandefur essentially regards the Privileges and Immunities and Due Process Clauses of the Fourteenth Amendment as guaranteeing the same rights: those of the declaration, which, even in their supposed indefiniteness, he regards as too limited: "It is unfortunate that by using the plural word 'rights,' the Declaration leads some readers to imagine freedom as broken up into discrete acts."[96] This certainly must be unfortunate to those who imagine the declaration guarantees all absence from interference, but the fact is that the rights in the document are specific. Had it been intended to embody the libertarianism of Mill, who published *On Liberty* nearly eight decades later, it would not possibly have commanded the assent of a Congress comprised of states with established churches, morals legislation, and other interferences with liberty.

HARRY JAFFA'S "DECLARTUTION"

Harry V. Jaffa's book *Original Intent and the Framers of the Constitution: A Disputed Question* sought to incorporate the declaration into the Constitution through what Charles Cooper, a critic who dubbed the resulting fusion Jaffa's "declartution," has called the "paradoxical" claim that "a provision of the Constitution can be unconstitutional."[97] Jaffa's argument is that the declaration is America's genuinely founding document, the pristine and coherent principles that constituted us "one people"—this despite that the declaration's reference to "one people," like the Constitution's to "We the People," implies it preexisted the document—whereas the Constitution was a jumble of compromises whose principles are often difficult to discern. Consequently, when a provision of the Constitution contradicts the declaration's tenet of equal rights to life, liberty, and the pursuit of happiness, the declaration should prevail.[98] As Cooper notes, this rests largely on an exceedingly strained reading of Madison's recommendation that the declaration be included in the curriculum of the University of Virginia. Madison had actually said the Declaration of Independence, while important to read, was of little use in construing the Constitution and that *The Federalist*—which Jaffa does not and, given its allusive defenses of the slavery provisions, cannot accord canonical status—was definitive.[99]

Bork's critical review of the famously irascible Jaffa sparked a war of essays in which both commentators said original intent was authoritative, but in which Jaffa said the original intent of the Framers assumed the natural law foundations of the declaration. Jaffa regarded it as heretical, which is to say un-Lincolnian, that Bork rooted rights in "historical experience" rather than "general theory."[100] But the passage from Lincoln that Jaffa offers for refutation does not accomplish its task. In it, Lincoln declares that "[p]ublic opinion on any subject always has a 'central idea' from which all its minor thoughts radiate." But Bork does not deny these central ideas or the fact that other principles can be deduced from them. The question is their source, which Bork, like Burke, finds in tradition. Nothing in this passage from Lincoln contradicts such an approach. Jaffa miscasts Bork—the author of *Slouching Towards Gomorrah: Modern Liberalism and American Decline*[101]—as a wholesale nihilist for whom all of politics is no more than irrational or emotional preference.

Jaffa further accuses Bork of "studiously ignor[ing]" the "distinction between the principles of the Constitution and its compromises." But its compromises—just like what Peter Lawler correctly notes are the legislative compromises that produced the declaration, which included the reference to "Nature's God" that Jaffa freights with such meaning—are authoritative precisely because they were posited and because the document would never have been adopted without them.[102] The moral obligation of promise-keeping entails respecting them. We may observe, for example, that Madison felt the equality of state representation in the Constitution flagrantly violated the principle of popular rule, which the declaration incorporates, so much so that he would only defend it in *Federalist* no. 62 as a naked compromise necessary to achieving consensus on the document.[103] But the constitutional provision that no state may be deprived of its equality in the Senate without its consent is no less binding. It would be startling were the Supreme Court to order a recomposition of the Senate by population on the grounds that its original structure violated the foundational law of the declaration.

Jaffa, like Sandefur, is given to the *reductio ad constitutionem*. His analysis is deformed by its almost unswerving limitation to the example of slavery, which is inescapable in American constitutionalism but which does not define every issue therein. It would be better to allow the likes of Madison to be accountable for the fullness of their virtues and sins than to derange their work. But Jaffa's *reductio* does not stop there. He writes, for example, that positivism would entail judicial enforcement of a law ordering Jews to wear yellow stars, as if judges would be adequate to rescue a society descended to that stage of corruption. The crucial point, as with Arkes, is that natural law arguments, including those grounded in the Declaration of Independence, are *political* claims, not judicial ones. Jaffa's hypothetical about yellow stars is inattentive to the fact that a society that passes such a law has already failed its natural law obligations. Positivism claims only that judges are bound to what the community posits. It does not prevent arguments grounded in natural law from being made in elected forums. Indeed, many leading positivists, Bork included, have urged exactly such arguments. What Jaffa overlooks is the nobility of a community freely choosing these principles even if it is tardy in doing so. Jaffa himself recognizes this in noting that the antebellum antislavery movement "pursued its ends through the political process," including by reference to the principles of the declaration.

Bork had the better of this argument, including a convincing reply to Jaffa's characterization of positivism. Positivism does not equate to moral relativism. In the hands of judges, it is a question of authority alone, not a suggestion that the content of laws should be normless. Bork wrote:

> The Framers were not legal positivists for the very good reason that no one who makes law can be. The lawgiver must have ideas of right

and wrong that antecede the law he makes. The Framers wrote law, presumably embodying as much of their thinking on natural rights as prudence allowed, and the judge is bound to follow the law no matter what he thinks of its correspondence to natural law. That means that, in his judicial capacity, though in no other, the judge must be a legal positivist.

Finally, it bears remarking that, like Arkes, Jaffa follows libertarian premises to conservative conclusions. Whereas Sandefur praises *Lawrence v. Texas*'s nullifying of state bans on homosexual sodomy, Jaffa is perfectly comfortable saying that "[s]odomy has always—hitherto—been regarded as an unnatural act, and a violation of natural law." Does that "always" suggest a deference to tradition? And on Jaffa's logic, ought the Court have *imposed* bans on homosexual intimacy where they did not exist? That would violate the central principle that arises from the declaration's commitment to equality: self-government. So does Jaffa's "Declartution."

THE JURISPRUDENCE OF NATURAL LAW

Hadley Arkes may seem an unusual object of commentary in a chapter critiquing judicial engagement. He has, after all, been a penetrating critic of the Court, especially where it attempts to resolve social and cultural controversies and does so almost always in the name of liberating individuals from traditional morality. In 1996, he participated in a symposium in the journal *First Things* that targeted "the judicial usurpation of politics." But Arkes's essay was largely silent on the question of judicial *authority*; what concerned him was less the fact that the Court had usurped democratic politics than the conclusions it had reached, especially on abortion and homosexuality, in doing so. [104] His treatment of George Sutherland, one of the justices who opposed New Deal reforms—and who, on Arkes's account, was willing to transcend the Constitution to reach its moral premises—suggests a similar conclusion.[105]

Arkes's magisterial *Beyond the Constitution* would direct the attention of jurists and other officials away from a literal, text-obsessed interpretation of the founding document and toward the moral logic of the law beneath it, which would be the same for all governments of all peoples in all places.[106] This sounds similar to Sandefur, but Arkes's conclusions fundamentally differ. On Arkes's reading, the only alternative to discovering this moral logic, as we have seen, is to reduce the law to a relativistic "habits of the tribe." Much of the actual text of the Constitution is unnecessary, Arkes argues, to its ends, which would be legitimate purposes of any authoritative government. Thus, for example, the maxim "innocent until proven guilty" appears nowhere in the Constitution and need not. Neither, then, need other elements of the logic and purposes of law be specified, such as those designed to secure accurate information (thus the prohibition on coerced confessions) or protect natural rights by prohibiting discrimination (thus the text of the Fourteenth Amendment, which had for Barnett revolutionized state-national relations, was actually unnecessary to authorize the national government to pursue ends to which it would have been empowered by the logic of law). Arising from logic, these principles are universal.

This universality recalls Immanuel Kant, yet Arkes's work also bears Aristotelian strains. But it is difficult to have both the goods of the untethered, abstract reason of a Kant and the prudence of an Aristotle. Prudence, for Aristotle as for Aquinas and Burke, is inseparable from both practice and particularity. The Kantian strain in Arkes stages an end run around the political life he otherwise values.

Arkes opens with an anecdote of a government lawyer searching, perhaps contorting, the constitutional text for authority to combat racial discrimination in private housing.[107] The lawyer's arguments were inventive, Arkes says, but missed the point: Racial discrimination is a wrong, and the national government possesses, by its nature and purposes, the ability to reach any wrong committed within its territory without reference to or contortion of constitutional text. Arkes appears to see something asinine or even corrupt in the gymnastics through which politicians and jurists go to apply the law without relying on its underlying principles, for which we must go, as his title indicates, "beyond the Constitution."

But Arkes overlooks something important in these interpretive exertions: the text is a force that binds a political community in which first principles can be instantiated. The lawyer whose contortions trouble Arkes is engaging in an exegetical exercise whose benefits are at least twofold. The first is an effort to discipline his own authority according to standards that are evident not just to philosophers or to philosophically minded jurists but also to the community that will submit to them. The second is that textual interpretation, much like biblical exegesis, reaches varied conclusions but on the basis of shared traditions. The fact that they are shared is itself a blessing to a community, for it speaks to our Aristotelian natures, draws us from our Tocquevillian shells and provides a common method for resolving disputes. Much of the richness of the Talmudic tradition Arkes cites consists in grappling with texts in a legalistic manner.

This shared quality of the text delineates a *particular* political community in which truths are to be acted upon. Leon R. Kass notes that in the Gettysburg Address, Lincoln—on Arkes's reading the preeminent statesman of natural law—repeatedly refers to "this" nation, using the word "here" no fewer than eight times.[108] Similarly, Lincoln's famous speech on *Dred Scott* accepted the decision's authority over the parties to the case even though he concluded it violated the moral logic of law, just as the Constitution's unfortunate clause on fugitive slaves remained in force for him because it had been posited. Lincoln repeatedly invoked the positive law of federalism, in which Arkes says no normative principle of natural or state authority can be discovered, to assure Southern states he had no intention of interfering with existing institutions of slavery, only of preventing its expansion.

Of course, these were prudential considerations aimed at the attainment of morally absolute aims, but prudence, too, is a cardinal virtue. Moreover, Lincoln articulated constitutional principles that dealt purely with the mechanisms rather than the rightness of political decisions. His Peoria Address's complaint with the Kansas-Nebraska Act was the heresy of repudiating the Missouri Compromise, which was authoritative because it had been posited by a particular political community. "The Missouri Compromise ought to be restored. For the sake of the Union, it ought to be restored. . . . If by any means, we omit to do this, what follows? Slavery may or may not be established in Nebraska. But whether it be or not, we shall have repudiated—discarded from the councils of the Nation—the SPIRIT of COMPROMISE; for who after this will ever trust in a national compromise? The spirit of mutual concession—that spirit which first gave us the constitution, and which has thrice saved the Union—we shall have strangled and cast from us forever."

It was the mechanism of that compromise—majority rule—that Lincoln endorsed in his first inaugural address: "From questions of this class [rights] spring all our constitutional controversies, and we divide upon them into majorities and minorities. If the minority will not acquiesce, the majority must, or the government must cease. There is no other alternative; for continuing the government, is acquiescence on one side or the other." Lincoln in all this was profoundly controlled by the positive law of the Constitution. The Lincoln-Douglas debates are intelligible and important to us because they concern not just competing principles but also varying interpretations—one right, one wrong—of a shared text.

To be sure, biblical exegesis is authoritative because the text is understood by its explicators to be transcendent and true, and Arkes says the same of genuine law. In this way, like other advocates of engaged judges, Arkes holds a normative view of law that imposes on the word the conclusions he reaches. But his views on the logic of law lead Arkes to sweeping deductions about the authority of judges that do not account for their fallibility beyond his offering of occasional reflections that are not in dispute: the presence of moral disagreement, Arkes explains, does not indicate an absence of moral truth, and only those he stigmatizes as "positivists," "relativists," and "Philistines" believe otherwise. But there is an essential distinction between believing there are absolute truths and doubting the ability of those, particularly those invested with power, to identify them accurately and apply them fairly.

As Burke has shown us, reason on these topics has a particular propensity to become zealous or abusive by virtue of the extent of its self-confidence and the gravity of the stakes involved. A shared text anchored in a shared tradition is thus grounding. These traditions are not mere laws of the tribe; they represent the collected wisdom of a society's experience, the theater in which principle is combined with a rich variety of circumstances. Burke's conclusion is that this tradition is likelier to contain wisdom than the discrete powers of logic of a professor or judge at any one moment in time. It goes without saying that a local custom can be abusive or wrong, as was the Southern tradition of slavery, and that it ought to be condemned and legally addressed when it is. But history records ample instances, from Revolutionary France to the eugenic movement of American Progressives to the mechanized murder of Nazi Germany, of the learned reaching conclusions by means of antiseptic logic where moral intuitions accumulated in custom would have been far more restrained, if only because these intuitions also include the invaluable virtue of self-doubt rather than the perfervid sense of assurance that the use of logic one asserts to be everywhere and always true can provide.

It is also unclear where or how this departure from the constitutional text, and the accompanying search for the principles beneath its principles, breaks what appears to be a cycle of infinite regression. For Arkes, the Fourteenth Amendment was gratuitous with respect to racial discrimination because, as the first Justice Harlan argued, the Thirteenth had already barred not just enslavement but also its "badges and incidents,"[109] a concept Barnett carries to the point of defining "[a]ny unwarranted restrictions on liberty—whether personal or economic—[as] partial 'incidents' of slavery."[110] But on Arkes's account, it is equally unclear why the Thirteenth was needed, since slavery is an objective wrong and any government worthy of the name has the power to right it regardless of its positive law.

We may go further: a Constitution must posit some form of government, as a presidential over a parliamentary system, since we may presume that natural law does not dictate such conclusions. But need it specify mechanisms for maintaining the separation of powers, long understood—through, not incidentally, conclusions Montesquieu derived by examining an organic, evolved British constitution that was not the product of instantaneous reason—to be essential to the individual's natural right to be free from arbitrary power? For example, Madison demonstrates with impeccable logic in *Federalist* no. 48 that maintaining the actual separation requires some mixture of powers such that the branches of government can repel one another. Suppose, then, that the Constitution did not equip the branches with checks, such as not specifying a presidential veto. Could a president have traveled beyond the Constitution to discover one? At what point does the entire fact of a written Constitution simply give way to the postulates of professors? What, for that matter, justifies any national borders that impose any particularity on the expression of law whose logic is universal? We might, in the vein of resisting such extremities, take one more step, which is to note that it is the positive law that induces reflections as to the rights and wrongs that precede it. Arkes's own admirable reverence for the Constitution and his filial piety toward the first generation of jurists, such as John Marshall, who explored its axioms suggest he is more beholden to "the local tribe" than his detached reason would suggest.

None of this is to say that serious inquiry into natural law should not be a part of our political conversation. Robert P. George, an eloquent exponent of natural law, agrees with Arkes and Jaffa that the Constitution is rooted in natural law and natural rights. But he notes that a judicial authority over such matters does not follow from this observation. "This is because the Constitution, as I read the document, places primary authority for giving effect to natural law and protecting natural rights to the institutions of democratic self-government, not to the courts, in circumstances in which nothing in the text, its structure, logic, or original understanding dictates an answer to a dispute as to proper public policy."[111] Similarly, Kramer questions whether the Founding generation shared this view of natural law being authoritative beyond the Constitution: "[W]hile few lawyers in the eighteenth century doubted either the existence of natural law or the importance of nature as a source of rights, these rights were rarely conceived as having positive authority independent of their incorporation into fundamental law."[112]

Arkes's earnest effort to protect natural rights is in tension with another natural right, *the* natural right for the Founders, which is self-government by a political community. The complex web of balances that must be struck here cannot be settled by the reason of judges or philosophers. It is thus deeply unfair to call Bork a moral relativist because he insists that the law be posited with identifiable signs of sufficient clarity for a judge to interpret with a reasonable claim of objectivity. The problem with Arkes in this sense distills to one of authority: not whether natural law should be invoked, but who should invoke it and how. That Arkes appeals consistently to the American regime rather than a cosmopolitan one is evidence of this tension. Beyond the Constitution lies a detached and antipolitical realm that unmoors individuals from the res publica, with all the attendant propensities for abuse such a move entails.

THE DUTY OF CLARITY

The role McGinnis would assign to judges is more modest than the commentators we have thus far encountered, but still not wholly so. His "duty of clarity"[113] would restrict judges to invalidating laws only in cases of a clear constitutional mistake. But he would not have them ascertain that from a posture of deference. Rather: "Jurists of the Founding era believed that even texts that might be unclear on their face or to a layperson could be clarified by interpretive methods and that these methods were reliable tools for discovering or establishing meaning. It was thus substantially less likely that the meaning of a provision would remain unclear after legal methods were applied."[114] Confronted with obscurity in legal meaning, judges should make a forthright effort to ascertain it using interpretive methods. Among the benefits of this approach for McGinnis is that it narrows the "construction zone" where normative principles exogenous to the text are applied because interpretation cannot ascertain a clear meaning. It is also preferable to James Bradley Thayer's standard that legislation should be overturned only where no rational person could see it as constitutional.

Thayer, of course, had suggested a standard of limiting judicial nullification to cases of a "clear mistake." It is probably more profitable to refer to McGinnis as proposing a duty of "clarification," a locution he sometimes uses. Whereas Thayer would have judges stop and defer in the face of unclarity, and those at the opposite end would have judges enter the construction zone, McGinnis would apply canons of interpretation accepted at the Founding to clarify what the Constitution means. Thus judges should aim, with far-reaching methods, to clarify meaning rather than use the equivalent of a legislative power to create it. This duty of clarity or of clarification is intrinsically embodied in the concept of judicial review. McGinnis and Michael B. Rappaport have called this "original methods originalism," the idea that "the Constitution should be interpreted using the interpretive methods that the constitutional enactors would have deemed applicable to it."[115]

McGinnis's obligation of clarity is a useful middle path between extreme deference and extreme engagement. The difficulty with the resulting "legal turn" in constitutional analysis is that it ignores the Constitution's status as a political document with a legal character and instead turns it over to the supervision of experts. Justice Joseph Story had said the Constitution was "adopted by the people in its obvious, and general sense."[116] By contrast, it is difficult to see why public meaning originalism, according to which the Constitution should be understood as it was by those who ratified it, should be binding if the people, not having all been trained in the rigors of legal analysis, could not have known what they were ratifying. We are back at the problem of the tyranny of the learned. The power to interpret a document written in a technical language inaccessible to laymen but binding on them is substantial. The Paradox of Engagement recurs: Given normal human motives with respect to the use of power, what will restrain judges, belonging to a priesthood who alone can understand the law, from abusing theirs?

The answer to this paradox is republican constitutionalism. All the watchers will watch each other, with no exception carved out for judges.

5. Cases and Controversies

Our profound national commitment to free and open debate is not a license for the vicious verbal assault that occurred in this case. Petitioner Albert Snyder is not a public figure. He is simply a parent whose son, Marine Lance Corporal Matthew Snyder, was killed in Iraq. Mr. Snyder wanted what is surely the right of any parent who experiences such an incalculable loss: to bury his son in peace. But respondents, members of the Westboro Baptist Church, deprived him of that elementary right. . . . As a result, Albert Snyder suffered severe and lasting emotional injury. The Court now holds that the First Amendment protected respondents' right to brutalize Mr. Snyder. I cannot agree.

—Justice Samuel Alito[1]

All Marine Lance Corporal Matthew Snyder's father sought was what Justice Alito called "a few hours of peace" to bury his son. Common sense or, failing that, common decency would seem to protect so modest a goal, but the Westboro Baptist Church and, eventually, eight justices of the Supreme Court disagreed. The church's leader, Fred Phelps, a fanatic and hatemonger who believes God is, as the Court put it, "punish[ing] the United States for its tolerance of homosexuality," organized a picket of Corporal Snyder's funeral featuring such signs as "God Hates the USA/Thank God for 9/11," "God Hates Fags," "You're Going to Hell," and "God Hates You."[2]

Albert Snyder sued under a tort called "Intentional Infliction of Emotional Distress," winning a verdict for millions of dollars in damages. Appealing the verdict, the church disputed neither its intentional vileness nor the emotional damage it inflicted on the Snyder family. Rather, Phelps sought refuge in the First Amendment, claiming the church was bringing attention to matters of public concern and that he consequently should not be held accountable for the distress the demonstration caused private mourners grieving a son who was killed in the line of military duty in Iraq. The Supreme Court, fully "engaged" and zealous for individual rights, responded with an 8-1 verdict in Phelps's favor, noting that the "'content' of Westboro's signs plainly relates to broad issues of society at large. . . . While these messages may fall short of refined social or political commentary, the issues they highlight . . . are matters of public import."[3]

None of this was in dispute either. But Justice Alito recognized what republican constitutionalism does but what the Court did not: This case did not concern merely Phelps's isolated right to speak bombastically and obnoxiously. It concerned competing rights, as nearly all assertions of rights do. Alito's compelling dissent noted that the church could have conveyed its message in any number of ways and in any number of forums that did not disrupt a private ceremony of mourning. Adjusting the boundaries of each party's rights would simply have entailed the protestors shouting their slogans elsewhere, in the inflammatory manner that never fails to bring the Westboro church the publicity it craves. It was true, he wrote, that the church members were addressing public matters and had a right to do so with whatever vehemence they chose. "It does not follow, however, that they may intentionally inflict severe emotional injury on private persons at a time of intense emotional sensitivity by launching vicious verbal attacks that make no contribution to public debate."[4]

Alito's perceptive dissent illustrates the avenues of sensible reasoning that are opened when we acknowledge what each of us knows, which is that rights are political things pertaining to political life, where they often conflict with one another. A perspective that denies this—that is blind to the ontological status of political community—cannot see the balance of rights that this case needed to strike. No one was suggesting prior restraint of the Westboro Baptist Church, only accountability for what it said and how it behaved. This is the kind of common-sense issue ordinary citizens serving on a jury or voting for their representatives have no difficulty sorting out. Why do judges?

One reason is that rights have become instruments of isolation rather than assertions presented and balanced in political life. Even John Stuart Mill recognized, by the end of *On Liberty,* that most of our outward actions affect others, a fact of human existence so clear, one that most people grasp so instinctively, that it would be tempting to follow the Declaration of Independence and call it self-evident were it not so obscure to so many scholars of law. When rights are in conflict, they must be adjusted to one another, and the community's paramount right is to govern itself according to its best judgment and local customs. That is not to say the community should always prevail. Quite often, prudence counsels light governance and tolerance. Moreover, as John O. McGinnis has correctly noted, liberty is part of American tradition.[5] But these are political arguments that should be politically asserted and resolved, not removed from the community's jurisdiction by means of transfer to the courts.

Mary Ann Glendon has taught that transforming all talk into rights talk—the mode of political dispute that uses claims of rights to short-circuit and delegitimize political conversation—is hostile to a shared life in which we are able to accommodate one another without isolating ourselves.[6] Justice Alito reminds us that even when rights are involved, they are almost never the claims of the solitary individual alone. Rights chafe, compete, and collide with one another. Moreover, when they are simply asserted without a commonly recognized basis, there is no mechanism for resolving them. That seems intentional: rights talk is meant to be a showstopper, invoked when we no longer want to converse but rather want merely to assert.

Yet James Madison's notion of the Bill of Rights as a common basis for appealing to the community reminds us both of the political nature of rights and of the importance of the common language that the fundamental but also positive law of the Constitution provides. That commonality is what enables the resolution of disputes over rights by means of civility, accommodation, and obligation, which includes the nobility of being willing to curb our own individual preferences to enable a shared and meaningful life. An individualist constitution can only see Fred Phelps. A republican constitution understands that he is part of, and obliged to, a political community. That, at bottom, is what republican constitutionalism is about.

Republican constitutionalism is characterized by several premises.

First and most important, the judiciary no less than the other branches is subject to the separation of powers. Rather than the linear model that rankled Madison, in which the constitutional process terminates in the judiciary, separation of powers would facilitate an ongoing conversation over time concerning constitutional meaning, one filtered through the people's representatives. Congress would thus not be reluctant to use the ample tools at its disposal for brushing judges back from rulings that intrude on policymaking. While it is the persuasive doctrine of *Marbury v. Madison* that the Court says what the law is and is duty bound to emphasize constitutional over statutory provisions, it does not follow that this power is the supreme or final word on the Constitution.[7]

The foremost of these tools is jurisdiction stripping, the use of Congress's authority to remove some cases from judicial cognizance. Congress's reluctance to deploy this clearly stated Article III power more frequently and forthrightly is striking. As we have seen, Hamilton endorsed its use. Yet when a raft of bills in the early 1980s sought to remove the Court's jurisdiction from a variety of "social" issues, the president of the American Bar Association—a group with a professional interest in the preservation of judicial authority, and one almost certainly affected by the professional narcissism that cannot see the capacity of anyone outside its trade as competent to constitutional questions—called them "the most serious constitutional crisis" since the Civil War.[8] This was comical hyperbole: the use of a clearly articulated constitutional authority can hardly be called a constitutional crisis, and even if the label fit, to call that—rather than anything that, for example, the Court has done—the most serious crisis since the Civil War was a vapid and manic rhetorical act. Congress's failure to pass such bills with any frequency is evidence either of the legislature's deliberate nature—it does not act immediately on public outrage over decisions—its timidity, or its desire to remain on a judicial chain, but in any of these cases, the threat of a constitutional crisis materializes only if judicial finality is an essential feature of the constitutional system.

Congress has several other tools short of the difficulty of constitutional amendment in polarized times. The size of the Court is Congress's choice—following Akhil Reed Amar, perhaps an even number of justices would help restore judicial humility—and the composition of the Court is something to which the Senate must consent. It is well within senatorial rights to interrogate the judicial views of nominees to the bench. The advice-and-consent power does not relegate the Senate to the status of a human resources department for the executive, merely checking qualifications. It is a substantive, meaningful power.

Congress can also pass laws that challenge rulings, as it did with the Religious Freedom Restoration Act of 1993, which corrected what legislators concluded was the lax standard of review of laws affecting religious practice that the Court elucidated in *Employment Division v. Smith*.[9] Relentless challenges—indeed, even the occasional use of some of these tools—may have a cumulative prophylactic effect of causing the Court to curb the scope of its rulings to avoid, as it generally prefers, confrontations with the political branches that it does not believe it can win. Since the Court knows it has only judgment rather than force or will, judicial audacity is likely only against a background of political passivity. In this regard, the president should not ignore specific rulings but can confine the scope of their application. Lincoln's successors can follow his example by respecting rulings only with respect to the parties to a case and declining to treat them as general precedents on the basis of a single decision—a tactic that would compel precedents to accrete more slowly rather than being handed down in toto from a judicial Sinai. In such efforts, republican constitutionalism demands of elected representatives of the people that they take constitutionalism seriously rather than pursuing their policy aims unreservedly and outsourcing questions of fundamental law to the courts.

As we have seen, *The Federalist* also identifies impeachment as "a complete security" against persistently abusive judges. Since the abortive impeachment of Justice Samuel Chase in 1804 and 1805, an informal precedent has held that judges cannot be impeached for their rulings, only for corruption.[10] In reality, the constitutional standard for judicial tenure is not simply "high crimes and misdemeanors" but also "good behavior." The problem with the failure to impeach judges for exceeding their authority is not that it does not happen frequently, but rather that judges regard it as inconceivable. A restoration of the original understanding of judicial impeachment, like the judicious use of these other tools, would serve a preventive effect. Judges should not live in fear, but neither should they be untouchable. As Matthew J. Franck, noting that Joseph Story shared Alexander Hamilton's views even well after the Chase impeachment, observes: "Impeachment may be awkward, impracticable, and generally undesirable—who could desire a remedy for judicial abuse that can be invoked too conveniently?—but if Hamilton is to be taken at his word, it is clearly available to Congress in the event that the judiciary strays too far from its 'strict rules and precedents.'"[11]

Congress must also be willing to do its own constitutional work rather than outsource it to the Court. When President Obama issued an executive order on immigration in 2014, Representative James Clyburn's reaction to complaints about its constitutionality typified the legislative attitude: "Let's let the courts decide whether it's constitutional. That's not for Congress to decide, that's why we have the courts to make that decision."[12] But members of Congress swear an oath to "support and defend the Constitution of the United States against all enemies, foreign and domestic; [to] bear true faith and allegiance to the same." Their duty to uphold the Constitution as they interpret it is no less than that of judges. For similar reasons, Congress must recover its capacity and, perhaps equally important, will to legislate with precision rather than delegating to administrators. The controversy over President Donald J. Trump's ban on immigration from several Muslim-majority countries arose in the first place because Congress had, in a 1952 law, delegated authority to the executive to make such decisions. Senate Majority Leader Mitch McConnell expressed constitutional concerns about President Trump's order but said that "ultimately it is going to be decided in the courts as to whether or not this has gone too far."[13] That could be so only because Congress is lax or craven. If it had objected to the order, it could have withdrawn or conditioned the delegation.

For their part, judges should act with restraint insofar as any constitutional officer should take a moderate view of his or her powers. The debates of the First Congress are rife with consideration of constitutional questions rather than ones of policy alone. For the first several decades of the republic, presidents used their veto powers primarily for constitutional reasons rather than merely to shape policy. Judicial modesty is a virtue in the sense that all political modesty is a virtue, but it cannot be normless. It requires a standard. While I have criticized its full applications above, McGinnis's rule of the clear mistake—a direct standard that obviates the need for either judicial construction or tiers of analysis made famous or infamous by footnote four of *United States v. Carolene Products*[14]—is a compelling one that moderates between extreme deference and extreme activism, provided it also includes both Hamilton's forward-leaning effort to understand laws in such a way that they are reconciled with the Constitution as well as a willingness of the other branches to use the weapons at their disposal to check judicial abuses.

Judges should also withdraw from the business of reviewing the rationality of laws as opposed to the rationality of the belief that they are constitutional. Larry D. Kramer clarifies the issue: "The critical thing to understand about rational basis scrutiny is that it was a rule of judicial restraint, not substantive constitutional law. It did not mean that laws were constitutional if they were rational."[15] If the Court insists on reviewing substantive rationality, it must acknowledge the legislature's authority to use custom and morality as rational bases for law because they encode the wisdom of ages rather than the impulses of the moment. Finally, for reasons the politics of obligation illuminate, judges should seek clarity in the positive fundamental law of the Constitution, not because what is posited is necessarily just but rather because it helps to constitute a political community and because its having been posited, agreed to, and sustained across generations forms Madison's "debt against the living."

The people, too, have a role to play. Franck has observed that "pleased or not [with the outcomes of the Court's decisions on constitutional controversies] they seem convinced that the Court is the right place to have them resolved."[16] Republican constitutionalism demands a revival not just of casual rhetoric of constitutional restoration but rather of a constitutional morality that includes serious reflection on questions of authority. It is unsurprising that the elected branches do not engage much in constitutional conversation given the fact that it has so little political salience. Republican constitutionalism requires that this change, that the people care not just that they do or do not get what they want, but also how policymaking occurs. Journalists can assist in such an effort by covering constitutional issues, including Court decisions and appointments, with more subtlety than merely reporting whose ox was or would be gored by a given ruling. Civic education must take the Constitution seriously and, importantly, treat it as a whole rather than simply rushing to the Bill of Rights. This is not a weak or throwaway solution. Distortions of civic education helped to induce the contemporary obsession with individual rights, and we should not underestimate the power of civic education well understood for reinvigorating political life under the Constitution.

Most of all, republican constitutionalism demands of citizens that they recognize the politics of obligation and the fact of common life. Citizens of a political community share space with others, and almost everything they do affects both some other individual and, more importantly, the moral and civic atmosphere of a community. Hence the civic-minded citizen will not casually resort to the judiciary to resolve dissatisfactions but will rather learn to live with them, confident in his or her ability to prevail on another issue on another day. There is a wide range of cases that could be resolved by common courtesy rather than constitutional dispute. Republican constitutionalism with an engaged public requires, for this reason, a return to Madison's politics of shifting factions in which no one belongs to a permanent majority or minority and hence has the magnanimity to prevail in political disputes with modesty and the confidence to lose with grace. The country's growing polarization, especially insofar as political identities increasingly depend on an affection for or antipathy toward the president, disrupt this system because citizens of a given political stripe agree immovably not just on one issue that affects them for one moment but on the full range of policy questions before the republic.

Republican constitutionalism is not designed to neuter the judiciary but rather to treat it like all the branches otherwise treat each other: as components of a system of separated powers. This system requires that all features of the separation of powers be operative. Presidents, for example, may check the judiciary by declining to lend the power of enforcement to its decisions, but presidents in turn must be checked by Congress, including by the power of impeachment. Any breakdown in this system imperils the totality. Republican constitutionalism thus assumes it is robust.

We may now consider how the concept would apply in a sampling of cases. This sampling is not intended to be exhaustive, only to illuminate different dimensions of republican constitutionalism. Thus, for example, the *Slaughter-House Cases* show how the Court properly declined to make the Fourteenth Amendment a standard for the evaluation of every state police power. *Brown v. Board of Education* provides an illustration of the Court properly acting in the face of a clear violation, as does *Citizens United v. Federal Election Commission*. The discussion of *Williamson v. Lee Optical*, a modern-day version of *Slaughter-House*, attempts to vindicate much maligned rational-basis review. What connects these and other cases is that they show how the Supreme Court should sometimes act—especially in cases of clear constitutional violations—and sometimes demonstrate Bickel's "passive virtues," always with an eye toward facilitating republican self-government.

THE *SLAUGHTER-HOUSE CASES*: PRIVILEGES AND IMMUNITIES

The *Slaughter-House Cases* raise the question of whether the Fourteenth Amendment so altered the relationship between the state and national governments as to make the traditional police power of local government subject to federal supervision, and judicial supervision at that.

The conventional wisdom about the case is that it denuded the Privileges and Immunities Clause of the amendment by imposing an artificial distinction between state and national citizenship, with Justice Samuel Miller, a Lincoln appointee, writing for a 5–4 majority that the amendment protects only the rights of the latter, not the former.

The cast of characters in the litigation, which concerned the State of Louisiana's attempt to regulate the New Orleans slaughterhouses whose filth had led to repeated cholera outbreaks by establishing a single monopoly facility for butchers to use, is an odd one for a case supposed to have gutted civil rights. The governor of Louisiana, Henry Clay Warmoth, was a Republican who served as a Union officer in the Civil War, who was elected with an African American lieutenant governor, and whose tenure witnessed the passage of antisegregation laws.[17] By contrast, the white butchers who sued were represented by John A. Campbell, a former justice who had resigned from the Supreme Court—during his tenure on which he had concurred in *Dred Scott*—in the wake of secession and returned to his Alabama home to become assistant secretary of war for the Confederacy. It is not too much to imagine that he saw this case as at least in part an opportunity to shift the focus of the Fourteenth Amendment, a bitter pill the southern states were compelled to swallow, away from its initial purpose of protecting formerly enslaved people.

As Kevin Newsom has argued persuasively, Miller's argument in *Slaughter-House* was not an attempt to gut the Privileges and Immunities Clause but rather to strike a compromise that incorporated the specific guarantees of the Bill of Rights while preserving the structure of federalism. The federalism issue for Newsom pertains to Campbell's argument for using the Fourteenth Amendment to transfer common-law economic rights, theretofore always subject to state regulation, to federal control.[18] Miller rejected this, and that is the import of his distinction between the rights of state and federal citizenship. It is true that Miller's opinion misstates the Privileges and Immunities Clause of Article IV, quoting it as guaranteeing the privileges and immunities of "citizens of the several states," when the clause actually refers to citizens "in" the several states.[19] But the weight that this misquotation can bear as evidence of malintent on Miller's part is limited by the fact that the first half of the sentence in Article IV does refer to "citizens of each state," and that the same construction ("citizens of the several states") was placed on Article IV by Justice Bushrod Washington in *Corfield v. Coryell.* Had the latter phrase ("citizens *in*") been a reference to federal citizenship, the Privileges and Immunities Clause of the Fourteenth Amendment would have been superfluous.

Moreover, as Miller notes, the Fourteenth Amendment's distinction between federal and state citizenship is explicit: it states that people born in or naturalized in the United States are citizens of *both* the United States and their states of residence, whereas the Privileges and Immunities Clause of the amendment protects only the rights of "citizens of the United States." Miller's argument is that while the Fourteenth Amendment does give the federal government the authority to legislate with respect to protecting national rights against local incursion, it does not alter those rights with respect to matters that had always been understood to be within the purview of the police power of the states. This persuasive analysis, which is certainly no more labored a reading of the text than the majority opinion in *District of Columbia v. Heller,* which surgically detached the prefatory from the operative clause of the Second Amendment, seems less controversial than what exactly the privileges and immunities of national citizenship entail.[20]

The intent of the Fourteenth Amendment, Miller wrote further, must be understood in the context of the Civil War amendments generally. It was to assure "the freedom of the slave race, the security and firm establishment of that freedom, and the protection of the newly-made freeman and citizen from the oppressions of those who had formerly exercised unlimited dominion over him."[21] Miller seems historically justified in noting that while the amendment is not limited to African Americans, "it is just as true" that its intent was their protection. This seems exceedingly hard to deny, but Miller's argument does not depend on it. All that was required to sustain his conclusion was the observation that the traditional police powers of the states over such matters as public health remained privileges of state citizenship that the Fourteenth Amendment did not superintend. To argue otherwise "would constitute this court a perpetual censor upon all legislation of the States, on the civil rights of their own citizens, with authority to nullify such as it did not approve as consistent with those rights, as they existed at the time of the adoption of this amendment."[22]

The ratification debates evince no such intent for the Court to serve as a censor over all state laws, and indeed a contrary argument would bear the burden of claiming that federal authorities were in a better position to gauge the proper disposition of animal waste in the city of New Orleans than was the Louisiana legislature. This would have been the end of federalism and the rise of judicial supremacy over more or less all state laws—an especially problematic result since the Fourteenth Amendment explicitly assigns its enforcement power to Congress. A transfer of authority that sweeping, as opposed to authority over the limited rights of national citizenship for the purpose of protecting formerly enslaved people, would have excited substantial and perhaps insuperable opposition by the state legislators who ratified it, and not only those in the defeated South.

Justice Stephen Field authored the principal dissent. He correctly identified the issue: "whether the recent amendments to the Federal Constitution protect the citizens of the United States against the deprivation of their common rights by State legislation." The phrase "common rights" is significant. As Newsom notes, Campbell had used it to refer primarily to economic rights. But these rights, like others, are exercised in a political context, and the argument that Congress, much less the Supreme Court, was in a better position than the Louisiana legislature to assess the best means of preventing cholera outbreaks in New Orleans requires a significant faith in national authorities. We have no objective means, other than imposing a construction like the Presumption of Liberty on the text—which the text itself does not warrant—of identifying the scope of these "common rights" in the first place, much less the conditions for their limitation. Field could not give them any precise definition either. He acknowledged that the police power of the state over such issues as public health was broad so long as its regulations "are not in conflict with any constitutional prohibitions or fundamental principles."[23]

Which principles? Field seemed unable to specify. There was a test of means-end fit insofar as Field argued that if one corporation could slaughter without endangering public health, others subject to the same restrictions could too, which is the apparent basis for his claim that "sanitary regulations" were a "pretence" and "shallow."[24] Yet this claim that the monopoly was unnecessary to accomplish its ends was an argument of policy that a judge distant from the scene was particularly unqualified to assess, both because it was not his expertise and because he was not on the ground. In his dissent, Justice Joseph P. Bradley tried to specify the rights protected by the amendment as well: there were "traditionary" rights inherited from our "ancestors" that included Blackstone's "absolute right, inherent in every Englishman . . . of property, which consists in the free use, enjoyment, and disposal of all his acquisitions, without any control or diminution save only by the laws of the land."[25] This sounds very much like what Arkes dismissed as "the habits of the local tribe," but in any event, the law of Louisiana did speak here: it specified the terms under which butchers could operate in a city in which their practices otherwise constituted a threat to public health.

Bradley continued, deriving an apparently implied right to "adopt such calling, profession, or trade as may seem to him most conducive to that end. Without this he cannot be a freeman."[26] Yet he could not possibly have meant this as broadly as he stated it. He surely meant a "lawful" calling: one, in other words, compatible with the public good. The State of Louisiana had decided that unrestricted butchering whose waste drained or was dumped into the Mississippi River was inconsistent with the common good. Bradley ultimately claimed that it was unnecessary even to specify that citizens of the national government enjoyed "all the privileges of citizens," which included the privilege of buying and selling property, engaging in "lawful employment" and "resorting to the laws for redress of injuries, and the like."[27] Here again, he cannot fully have meant what he said. While he now specified that employment must be lawful, the same is true of buying, selling, and using property, all of which are subject to law. Buying medications without a prescription is a crime. So is selling prohibited drugs. Property can be zoned, and so forth.

Bradley would have held any state-sanctioned monopoly to violate the Privileges and Immunities clause, but Miller anticipated that argument in a passage important for republican constitutionalism. Campbell's argument had invoked opposition to state monarchies in England, a theme Field took up in detail, but Miller observed that the situation in the United States differed fundamentally. The complaints in England referred "to monopolies established by the monarch in derogation of the rights of his subjects, or [that] arise out of transactions in which the people were unrepresented, and their interests uncared for."[28] In other words, Campbell treated the government as many advocates of judicial engagement do: as a foreign object intruding on the rights of citizens, whereas the reality was that the people's interests were represented in a parliament in Britain—and legislatures in America—that did grant exclusive privileges like monopolies.

Of course, as the dissents argue, citizenship must have meaning. Miller, as Newsom shows, navigates a middle course between total abdication to whatever states wish to do on the one hand and judicial superintendence of all state laws on the other. By all signs, especially the illustrations of privileges and immunities he supplied, Miller was open to incorporation. It is inaccurate, then, to suggest that *Slaughter-House* vitiated the Privileges and Immunities Clause, something of which subsequent citations to the case, as in *Plessy v. Ferguson*, were guilty but of which Miller was not.

What Miller's republican constitution enables is not merely local discretion or control but also local responsibility and political life. The butchers were not isolated individuals: their trades affected the health and aesthetics of the community. The question of how best to address the cholera outbreaks and other problems is exactly the kind of concern that Alexis de Tocqueville said elicited local political involvement because it entailed not abstract or distant questions of government but rather ones that immediately touched people's lives. Tocqueville wrote of such concerns: "Only with difficulty does one draw a man out of himself to interest him in the destiny of the whole state, because he understands poorly the influence that the destiny of the state can exert on his lot. But should it be necessary to pass a road through his property, he will see at first glance that he has come across a relation between this small public affair and his greatest private affairs, and he will discover, without anyone's showing it to him, the tight bond that here unites a particular interest to the general interest."[29]

A reading of the Fourteenth Amendment compatible with the vitality of local political life must preserve some space for federalism, which is one of the preconditions for republican constitutionalism. Leaving states a wide berth for lawmaking induces participation in political life, including participation in questions of a constitutional character. When such decisions are routed upward to Congress, and even more so when they are simply transferred to the courts, political life erodes because the citizen's participation is diluted. Tocqueville saw the concentration of the citizen's participation as a central feature of the constitutional design: for America's Founders, "it was fitting to give political life to each portion of the territory in order to multiply infinitely the occasions for citizens to act together and to make them feel every day that they depend on one another."[30]

BROWN V. BOARD OF EDUCATION

To be sure, local power can be exercised abusively. In certain cases, the national political community has acted decisively to remove issues from local control. Racial discrimination is one of these. The framers and ratifiers of the Fourteenth Amendment concluded that local racial dominance and discrimination made it necessary to remove superintendence of these issues to the level of the nation. Attempts to expand its scope notwithstanding, it was the clear purpose of the Fourteenth Amendment to correct the problem of racial animus encoded in local policy. The clearest and best-known illustration of its proper application is *Brown v. Board of Education*.[31] But the particular reasoning used in *Brown,* which deployed social scientific evidence to demonstrate that segregation was harmful to children, left open the possibility that segregation could be legal if, somehow, its impact could be shown to be benign. The import of the Fourteenth Amendment is that the states are not allowed to discriminate on racial grounds simply, regardless of the discrimination's effect.

Justice Clarence Thomas identified the issue in his concurrence in the 1995 case of *Missouri v. Jenkins,* in which he disputed the suggestion that a school was inferior simply by dint of being predominantly African American. The Fourteenth Amendment, he argued, prevented de jure segregation, and the prohibition did not rest on a test of harm. "Indeed, *Brown I* itself did not need to rely upon any psychological or social-science research in order to announce the simple, yet fundamental, truth that the government cannot discriminate among its citizens on the basis of race."[32] The importance of *Brown* is that it illustrates a clear case in which the courts *should* act, not because local communities are wrong or even because they are unfair but rather because the national political community has made a deliberate determination to remove issues from their control. But it is also worth noting that actual desegregation followed not *Brown* but rather the Civil Rights Act of 1964. It is entirely possible that *Brown* helped to galvanize the 1964 Act, but Gerald Rosenberg has shown that the latter yielded more enduring movement on desegregation.[33]

The decisive fact about *Brown* is that the Fourteenth Amendment deliberately removed questions of racial discrimination from local governments, which were infected with racism and resistant to change. The Court's power arises in this case not from the inherent injustice of discrimination but rather from the political community's judgment that local institutions could not be trusted to uproot it. There are certainly instances of entrenched interests that resist change, but the Court is empowered to remedy the situation only when the Constitution nationalizes the issue. Importantly, the Court is not the only place to seek national relief when local politics is unavailing: the Civil War amendments all empower Congress to enforce their provisions legislatively. Regardless, the Court does not wield an abstract power to right all wrongs, only those that the Constitution clearly places under national jurisdiction. To argue that the Court should step in where politics fails is to run up the white flag on republicanism in favor of judicial guardianship. It is certainly true that local politics can be nasty and brutish, but so can national politics. If problems cannot be solved face to face, the problem is not with the authority of courts but rather with republicanism itself.

Still less does the Court have a free-range power to correct foolish or even corrupt laws. It is in this context that we consider what is, for proponents of judicial engagement, one of the most controversial cases of modern times: *Williamson v. Lee Optical.*

REHABILITATING *LEE OPTICAL*

The 1955 case of *Williamson v. Lee Optical Co.* utilized a standard according to which legislation need not prove itself to be "logically consistent with its aims" to withstand judicial scrutiny. Rather, it could stand as long as "there [was] an evil at hand it might be thought that the particular legislative measure was a rational way to correct it."[34] Randy Barnett among others believes *Lee Optical* establishes an irrebuttable presumption in favor of legislation, since those who challenge it cannot be expected to foreclose any or every conceivable basis for it.[35] This talk of rationality has led to comparisons to James Bradley Thayer's famous or, depending on one's perspective, infamous dictum that "whatever choice is rational is constitutional."[36] But Thayer referred not to whether the legislation was a rational means of achieving its ends but rather whether it was rational to believe it was constitutional. We shall see that the difference is important.

Lee Optical concerned an optician who wanted to sell eyeglasses directly to the public in what has been described as an early precursor of the business model of Lenscrafters. The model violated a flagrantly special-interest law of Oklahoma that required a prescription from an ophthalmologist or optometrist before an optician could so much as replace a broken lens. We may stipulate that the law was a mere attempt by a licensed class to limit access to their trade, much like the licensing rules for florists or hair-braiders about which Neily wrote. The question

is whether that made it unconstitutional as opposed to unwise, irrational, or even corrupt. Justice William O. Douglas wrote for a unanimous
majority that the legislature may have had many motives for choosing
this particular means to achieve an appropriate end of public health and
safety, and it was for the legislature to weigh their pros and cons. But ultimately, the actual motive did not matter so long as a rational basis for
the law was conceivable. Thus "[w]e cannot say that the regulation has
no rational relation" to the objective to maintain the professionalism of
eye care.

This is an unfortunate locution of the standard. To say a law can
only be overturned if it is irrational to consider it unconstitutional—
Thayer's standard—is different from making the Court the judge of the
rationality of laws as measured by their means-end fit. On this reading,
the objection to *Lee Optical* is not the method of the case but rather that
the presumption of rationality at which it arrives cannot be answered.
Thayer's standard is also difficult to meet, but they differ in kind. Thayer's simply restates, perhaps in extreme form, Hamilton's assurance that
the judiciary could only void a law at "irreconcilable variance" with the
Constitution. But Douglas, like Barnett, would have made judges the arbiters of the link between means and ends—a link populated by a range
of prudential choices for any given policy—even as it set that bar so low
that virtually any statute could pass it.[37]

The case could have been disposed of simply by saying that if the
regulation was objectionable it was a responsibility of republican politics
to correct it. Even if it was motivated solely by corrupt motives—and we
have already seen that few enactments have neat, square-cornered motivations—the courts were not the proper forum for resolving the dispute.
Proponents of judicial engagement would doubtless answer, as many do,
that such breezy assurances ignore the reality of unseemly rent-seeking
that occurs in the nooks and crannies of legislative behavior, a process
of which few citizens can possibly be aware. Even worse, the sheer scale
of regulatory activity in the modern state makes it impossible, perhaps
even irrational, for a voter to cast his or her sole ballot based on any single one of them unless, of course, the voter is a beneficiary. Rent-seeking

activity almost always redounds to the benefit to its practitioners rather than those who bear its diffuse costs.

But the problem is not the scale of rent-seeking activity, but rather the nature and scale of government activity. These nooks and crannies, which are products of the complexity of the modern state, inevitably breed rent-seeking and factious behavior. If the nooks and crannies exist because the state is micromanaging economic outcomes at all—not just with respect to eyewear—interest-group horse trading and rent-seeking are inevitable. The solution is structural: It is to simplify, which is different from "shrink," government, thereby closing off the spaces in which rent-seeking thrives. Put otherwise, the problem with rent-seeking is not the seeking of rents but rather the provision of them. This is not an argument for small or large government. Government can be small and complex or large and simple. The point is merely that an ethic of simple government would have driven the Oklahoma legislature out of the business of micromanaging the fitting of eyewear in the first place.

This is, of course, idealistic. But a community's ideals are achieved or, better put, approximated in political forums, not by judicial fiat. The approach of judicial engagement would actually discourage efforts to simplify government by cleaning up the messes rent-seeking leaves, relieving citizens and legislators of the burden of doing so—often at political cost—themselves. It is an ideal that will never be approximated so long as judges are "perpetual censors" of legislation, the easy fix that supplants the hard work. What is needed to encourage this is not a standard of review that permits anything that can be shown to be rational. That already accepts the many assumptions embedded in Douglas's implication that if a law *were* wholly irrational, judges would be justified in voiding it for that reason. Yet it is not clear that they would be, or that any law can be so irrationally linked to its end as to fail the test.

A presumption of constitutionality, a well-credentialed standard whose advocates included Hamilton, Marshall, and Bushrod Washington, was more than adequate to dispose of the case—and, more important, sufficient to stimulate people properly outraged by the legislature's behavior to assert themselves politically and urge not just a reversal of this policy but a withdrawal from the inherently factious activity of picking economic winners and losers. This political assertion, whether it involved petition drives or public awareness campaigns, would have drawn the opticians of Lee Optical—small entrepreneurs who stood utterly alone against the state in court—into company with their fellow citizens where, in Tocqueville's phrase, the heart could be enlarged by the action of men on one another. The effect of the standard in *Lee Optical* was not to validate rent-seeking but rather to force the legislature to be accountable for it.

GLOUCESTER COUNTY SCHOOL BOARD V. G.G.: THE JURISPRUDENCE OF EMPATHY

A more recent case, which nearly required resolution at the Supreme Court and may still, involves a young person named Gavin Grimm—known in the case *Gloucester County School Board v. G.G.*[38] by initials to protect a then-minor's identity—who was born biologically female but identifies as male. Grimm, who publicized the case and thus emerged from anonymity, sought to use the boys' bathroom at school. When the school board declined, the Obama Administration threatened it with a loss of federal funding under Title IX. The Education Department had issued guidance interpreting that law, which guarantees men and women equal access to educational activities, as applying to gender identity and not just biological sex. Under the Supreme Court's precedent in *Auer v. Robbins*,[39] an agency is entitled to deference in interpreting its own regulations.

This is an instance of deference that undermines republican constitutionalism because it facilitates an escape from political to administrative activity. Making, as it were, a federal case out of it distorted the issues in the case by seeming to erect a battle between a transgender youth and what the avant garde understanding would regard as an oppressive school board. Yet while Grimm handled the lawsuit with dignity and courage, the youth, seeking empathy, showed little for others in the community who might reasonably be distressed at sharing a bathroom with someone with different intimate anatomy. Grimm described the issue as one of "common sense," thus placing opponents outside the boundaries of rational discourse.

In an essay in the *Washington Post*, Grimm asked the Supreme Court to "see me and the rest of the transgender community for who we are—just people—and rule accordingly."[40] Certainly the Court should respect all people's humanity, which no one in Grimm's case had denied. But courts are to rule according to laws. Grimm's understanding verged on a jurisprudence of empathy. It is as much as calling for the rule of emotion and not laws. The case—which was derailed on its path to the Supreme Court when the Trump Administration changed the Education Department policy that had sparked it—illustrates its perils. There are at least two parties to all controversies that come before the Court, and to seek empathy for one side is to reject it for the other, in this case a school board representing parents and children whose concerns may or may not have been right but were certainly not contrary to "common sense."

What Grimm failed to realize is the fact of our political natures. We assert rights in communities in circumstances in which they almost always affect others. The ideal way to resolve the situation—barring an informal accommodation, which Grimm rejected as "stigmatizing and unnecessary"—would have been republican constitutionalism: the family could persuade the community of the justice of the case, something that should have been that much easier if it was a matter of common sense. This assumes, of course, that people are reasonable, especially when confronted with the human face of controversial issues. But the alternative to that assumption is giving up on republicanism in favor of a judicial protectorate, enlightened members of which will not always be at the helm.

This openness to politics is closed off when administrative agencies that are antipolitical by deliberate design receive excessive deference, as they do under both *Auer v. Robbins* and *Chevron v. Natural Resources Defense Council,* the latter of which establishes a presumption in favor of an agency's interpretation of a statute.[41] Curbing the power of courts is not an end in itself; stimulating the activity of legislatures, by contrast, more approaches the telos of political life. *Chevron* and *Auer* are standards that discourage legislative activity and clarity in favor of administrative decisions. Legislators tend not to weep over them because such arrangements allow them to claim broad and popular goals legislatively without being responsible for the hard choices involved in implementation. Republican constitutionalism would recognize that lawmaking is a political responsibility and that standards of deference to administrative agencies that actively deter legislative activity are suspect. Administrative deference discourages politics by undermining the authority of statutes passed by representatives of a deliberative and engaged people.[42]

DEFERENCE, PROPER AND IMPROPER: THE HEALTH CARE CASES

Chief Justice John Roberts's opinion in *National Federation of Independent Businesses v. Sebelius,* which sustained the Affordable Care Act's mandate that individuals purchase health insurance, has been widely denounced by proponents of judicial engagement, but it was a masterwork of republican constitutionalism. Roberts effectively cabined the Commerce Clause, providing a fifth vote to reject the argument that it could be used to compel participation in economic activity, but also said the mandate, which was enforced with a penalty, could be seen as a tax on people who do not carry insurance.

Critics, including the dissenting conservatives in the case, have said the penalty was obviously not a tax because Congress did not call it one. Yet Roberts persuasively suggested that the actual operation of the law, not the particular label affixed to it, should be scrutinized: "In effect, [the dissenters] contend that even if the Constitution permits Congress to do exactly what we interpret this statute to do, the law must be struck down because Congress used the wrong labels."[43] Roberts's opinion, which supplied a rationale for the law that the legislation itself did not contain, is an excellent illustration of a judge making an active effort to reconcile a law with the Constitution, which *Federalist* no. 78 requires.

From the perspective of republican constitutionalism, Roberts refused to rescue Congress from responsibility for the law: "The Affordable Care Act's requirement that certain individuals pay a financial penalty for not obtaining health insurance may reasonably be characterized as a tax. Because the Constitution permits such a tax, it is not our role to forbid it, or to pass upon its wisdom or fairness."[44]

Within six years of the decision, and after four national elections in which the Affordable Care Act remained a divisive issue, Congress repealed the penalty associated with the mandate. The arguments for repeal included assertions that it was unconstitutional. Regardless of how one feels about the mandate, that steady, deliberate pace of repeal better suits the natural tempo of constitutionalism than a one-time decision from the Court. Roberts in essence forced Congress to do its own work and accept the attendant responsibility.

By contrast, in *King v. Burwell*, Roberts's effort to save the Affordable Care Act by means of deference to the elected branches had the opposite effect.[45] The Act had provided tax credits for health care purchased on exchanges "established by the state." When, to policymakers' surprise, objecting states declined in large numbers to establish the exchanges, the IRS interpreted the law to encompass a national exchange. Roberts in effect terminated an ongoing political process in an attempt to salvage its initial results. The authors of the Affordable Care Act placed an obvious bet that did not hit: they believed the financial incentives in the bill would induce states to establish exchanges. They were wrong, but rather than attempting to legislate again—something that would have required accommodation to what was by then a Republican Congress—the Obama Administration attempted to redefine the plain meaning of words by administrative fiat. Prior to the Court's intervention, an intricate constitutional dance involving nearly every player in the system—states, Congress, the president, all representing the people from different perspectives—was playing out. The Court brought the music to a halt by endorsing a flagrant administrative misreading of a statute.

It might be objected that Roberts deliberately misread the penalty assessed on the individual mandate too. But the cases differ. In one, Roberts assessed the law as it operated, where only the choice of a synonym stood between it and a holding of constitutionality. "Penalty" is much closer to "tax" than "state" is to "federal." The first pairing are synonyms, the second, in constitutional parlance, are opposites. The larger difference between the two health care cases is that one facilitated republican self-government by sending a political controversy back to the political branches, while the other undermined republicanism by withdrawing an ongoing political dispute from the field. Deference is far more appropriate to congressional than to administrative policymaking because Congress, the prime agent of republican constitutionalism, is widely assumed best to represent the full and meticulous diversity of the public.

It may be objected that the realities of the modern administrative state are incompatible with empowering Congress in this way. It certainly is true that administrative agencies wield far more power than the Framers could have imagined, and it is equally true that the fullness of their authority is unlikely to—and probably should not—ebb. The issue is not that administrative agencies should be stripped of their power but rather that they should be subordinate to meaningful guidance from legislators. Congress does not have the authority to transfer legislative power to the executive branch. It clearly can delegate authority over details, such as the exact level of particulate matter allowable under the Clean Air Act. But the Court should require—as it did in *A.L.A. Schecter Poultry Corp. v. United States*[46]—that the delegation be accompanied by standards so that administrators are not making legislative decisions. The goal, again, should be to facilitate politics.

That is the same reason the Court has been correct repeatedly to overturn schemes that excessively regulate campaign finance, most controversially in *Citizens United v. Federal Election Commission.*[47]

CITIZENS UNITED: FACILITATING POLITICS

Citizens United nullified federal restrictions on corporate spending in elections, triggering widespread concern about corruption. But republican constitutionalism suggests a different lens for viewing the issue. Speech is both a political act and a facilitator of public engagement in the political process. Advocates of campaign finance reform are wont to note that the communications it subsidizes are not substantive, even that they repel voters. But it is not the business of Congress to police whether political conversation is sufficiently cultured to deserve constitutional protection. The basic problem with this position, aside from the fact that corruption is an artifact of the complexity of government, not of campaign finance, is that it views politics from the perspective of donors (what do they want?) and candidates (what do they get?) but never voters (what do they need?).

In this sense, *Citizens United* was rightly decided but poorly argued. It was concerned almost wholly with the isolated rights of the speaker and very little with the context of political life. The former concern sees speech as an autonomous, self-justifying right, a conversation that leads inexorably toward side controversies like whether corporations have rights. This controversy could call on reasonable arguments in either directions. There is ample evidence that the Founding generation was willing to regulate corporations differently from individuals; on the other hand, it is difficult to see why organization in the corporate form deprives individuals of rights they otherwise hold. Regardless, this deontological view of speech misses its teleological function of facilitating political activity. In Madison's description, the point of freedom of speech and press was to enable another right: that of "freely examining public characters and measures, and of free communication among the people thereon."[48]

Shifting our perspective from the individual rights of the speaker to the political duties of the audience, we are able to see that more speech is better for republicanism. Yes, some of it will be demagogic, outrageous, or misleading, but the alternative is for the state to police the quality of speech. The end of republicanism is better served by more speech than less, even if raising the absolute quantity of communications also increases the number of them that serve that purpose poorly. Justice William Brennan employed this teleological understanding of rights in

New York Times v. Sullivan, the case establishing the standard of actual malice for libel claims against public figures. According to Justice Brennan's majority opinion, the basis of the diminished protection for these figures is the telos—the purpose—of the First Amendment or, in his terms, the reason it was "fashioned." He wrote:

> The general proposition that freedom of expression upon public questions is secured by the First Amendment has long been settled by our decisions. The constitutional safeguard, we have said, "was fashioned to assure unfettered interchange of ideas for the bringing about of political and social changes desired by the people."[49]

Note Brennan's use of "unfettered," and the orientation toward the people, not fairness for the speaker or, in this case, even the target of speech that seems unjust or was, as in *Sullivan,* even demonstrably inaccurate. Yet the Supreme Court's campaign finance jurisprudence has gradually departed from this teleological understanding, substituting a deontological interpretation of the First Amendment according to which speech is a right, full stop, without reference to any other good. This must inevitably culminate in controversies like the one surrounding *Citizens United* because it can see only the right of the speaker to communicate rather than the real issue, which is the right of the community to as much information as possible with which to engage in political life. Limiting speech in the name of preventing corruption—corruption that is inevitable in any complex, micromanagerial regime that involves itself in the business of picking winners and losers—or promoting equality of speakers, which the First Amendment does not guarantee, has the effect of undermining political life. Republican constitutionalism would have oriented the case from the deontology of the speaker and toward the telos of the audience, thus placing *Citizens United* on a firmer basis.

Citizens United, like *Brown,* occupies a unique category because it pertains to a specific constitutional prohibition: the regulation of political speech, which the First Amendment explicitly removes from congressional jurisdiction. The claim here is not for a free-range judicial authority to police the proper functioning of democracy, which would invite judicial activism on left and right alike. John Hart Ely, for example, would license judicial review in cases in which those with power are "choking off the channels of political change" to block those without power.[50] As J. Harvie Wilkinson III notes, the power to define democracy is itself immense, and it lacks a "constitutional warrant." Wilkinson observes that "the Constitution at most gives judges specific authority to redress violations of specific prohibitions."[51] That specific prohibition, and not a generalized power to decide what democracy means or to open the path to political change, is what legitimates *Citizens United.*

THE FOURTEENTH AMENDMENT AND CONGRESSIONAL AUTHORITY

We have already seen that Congress responded to *Employment Division v. Smith* by legislating a standard of strict scrutiny for measures that substantially affected religious practice. In *City of Boerne v. Flores,* the Court struck the Religious Freedom Restoration Act down as it applied to the states.[52] Justice Anthony Kennedy's majority opinion "adopted a startlingly strong view of judicial supremacy."[53] The opinion asserted that Section Five of the Fourteenth Amendment, which gives Congress the power of enforcement, applied only to preventing or remediating but not defining violations of the amendment. The opinion's conclusion stated the point most starkly:

> When the Court has interpreted the Constitution, it has acted within the province of the Judicial Branch, which embraces the duty to say what the law is. When the political branches of the Government act against the background of a judicial interpretation of the Constitution already issued, it must be understood that in later cases and controversies the Court will treat its precedents with the respect due them.[54]

In other words, the Court claimed for itself the exclusive right under *Marbury* to interpret the law. But as Edward Corwin, Charles Hyneman, and Louis Fisher among other scholars have noted, *Marbury* does not proclaim an exclusive right of the judiciary to interpret the law.[55] Marshall says it is "emphatically the province and duty of the Judicial department to say what the law is." "Emphatically" does not mean "exclusively." The other branches routinely interpret the Constitution as, indeed, they must if they are to be even minimally conscientious about their work. Congress must have an interpretation of the Constitution to assert its enactments are permissible under it; the president interprets the Constitution in the course of enforcing it and laws enacted under it.

Kennedy's opinion in *City of Boerne* amounts to saying that the judiciary alone interprets the Constitution and the other branches operate within the boundaries the courts set. This would be a problem even in the absence of Section Five because it sets the judiciary apart from the separation of powers and makes it the superintendent of the other branches, but Section Five clearly assigns the relevant authority to Congress and not the courts. Our concern for purposes of republican constitutionalism is less the parameters of this case than the fact that Kennedy's standard would excuse Congress from any responsibility for constitutional interpretation. There is a sense, to be sure, in which Congress welcomes this flight from responsibility, but that impulse should not be encouraged. The framers of the Fourteenth Amendment manifestly expected Congress to involve itself in constitutional issues, which is the entire import of Section Five.

The Court looked past an identical enforcement section of the Fifteenth Amendment in *Shelby County v. Holder,* which voided two provisions of the Voting Rights Act providing for federal supervision of voting laws in states with a history of discrimination.[56] The Act had been reauthorized as recently as 2006 with a unanimous vote in the Senate and a nearly unanimous one in the House, including the representatives of the affected states, who evidently felt the provisions were still necessary. The Court said these parts of the law were unconstitutional because they did not correspond with contemporary discrimination as opposed to that which occurred in 1965, when the law was originally enacted. Yet especially where the Constitution explicitly gives Congress authority, the question is which branch of government is best situated to judge conditions on the ground. One need not agree with the provisions of the Voting Rights Act in question or believe any degree of voting discrimination does or does not occur to regard it as irrefutable that elected representatives from across the country—including, again, those from the aggrieved states—are better positioned than nine unelected judges to assess local conditions.

In oral argument, Justice Scalia, normally a proponent of reasonable deference to the political branches, turned this on its head, arguing that it was necessary for the Court to rescue members of Congress from the unpopularity of opposing voting rights. Attributing the continued—in fact, escalating—support for the Act to the "perpetuation of racial entitlement," Scalia offered a flagrantly political, in the sense of electoral, analysis: "I don't think there is anything to be gained by any Senator to vote against continuation of this act. And I am fairly confident it will be reenacted in perpetuity unless—unless a court can say it does not comport with the Constitution."[57] On Scalia's account, the very fact that the Act commanded widespread support was somehow proof that the support was insincere. But this is not for courts to judge: the only way the Constitution registers public opinion is through elections, which it then filters through the official acts of representatives. Political punditry by judges is no substitute. Even assuming Scalia was correct, the ruling was a gift to members of Congress who could indulge in the electoral benefits of supporting voting rights while an unelected court assured some of the most pivotal parts of the law would not be enforced.

These claims of exclusive title to the practice of constitutional interpretation on the one hand and judicial guardianship on the other suggest precisely what Brutus predicted, and what the Paradox of Engagement reflects. Judges are not immune to the temptations of unchecked power. Indeed, they have sought to reserve it to themselves even where the Constitution explicitly indicates otherwise.

LEAVING SPACE FOR POLITICS

Avoiding these ultimate conflicts over constitutional questions leaves space in which politics can operate, a point two recent cases—*Town of Greece v. Galloway* and *Masterpiece Cakeshop v. Colorado Civil Rights Commission*—illustrate.[58] Both were cases that, under an ethic of republican constitutionalism, never belonged in the courts and that consequently provide apt illustrations with which to conclude this study.

In *Town of Greece*, plaintiffs challenged the practice of a small and overwhelmingly Christian New York town of opening sessions of its town council with a prayer. After receiving complaints that the prayers were sectarian, the town made an effort to diversify those invited to lead them. Nonetheless, two individuals who remained offended sued, snatching the constitutional conversation from the political realm—in exactly the kind of small locality in which it could be most fruitful—and transferring it to the federal courts.

The purpose here is not to review the merits of the case, in which the Court ruled that legislative prayer has a long history and is constitutional as long as it is not coercive or connected with the allocation or denial of any public good, so much as to ask why a small town of presumably neighborly people were unable to strike a working compromise. Some of the prayers cited in the case were arguably stridently sectarian, but republican constitutionalism would have ultimately called on those offended to explain to their neighbors why they were, and on their neighbors to respond reasonably to their concerns. That is not to be Pollyannish: there are certainly unreasonable people, but we are likeliest to be civil when a personal face is put on a public issue, whereas our immoderation is likeliest to express itself in either conditions of anonymity like large-scale politics or when the community's right to decide an issue concerning itself is revoked and transferred to the courts.

The case could have been resolved by either side demonstrating the virtue of civility to the other. The most problematic aspect of the case is that neither side could find a way to accommodate the other without resorting to the courts. In dissent, Justice Elena Kagan argued that it was the very locality of the issue that would place pressure on individuals to conform. If that is the case, our capacity for political life is badly eroded and will not be restored by further removing issues from the res publica. Political life demands qualities and skills, civility foremost among them, that atrophy when not exercised. Our compulsion for converting every dispute into a question of rights is fundamentally antipolitical. As we have seen that Mary Ann Glendon teaches, it alienates neighbors from each other while pushing all issues to the extremes and discouraging—often fully delegitimizing—the compromises and sensitivities that are hallmarks of a healthy republican order.

Those qualities were nowhere to be seen in *Masterpiece Cakeshop*, which involved a Colorado baker, Jack Phillips, who refused on religious grounds to provide a cake to celebrate the wedding of a gay couple. The couple subsequently turned to the Colorado Civil Rights Commission, which ruled against Phillips, who then appealed to the federal courts. Each side had a reasonable constitutional argument. In the end, the Court sided with Phillips 7–2 on narrow and fact-specific grounds that pertained to expressions of animus toward Christians by Commission members, but the real question is why the case required the resolution of authorities when informal mechanisms of society ought to have been wholly adequate to it. It is clear as day that no couple wants a wedding cake from a baker who disapproves of their union. This ought to have been a question of neighborliness, not law. The informal mechanisms available included going up the street to another baker, which would have resulted in Masterpiece Cakeshop losing business. The use of legal mechanisms to challenge him was not about civil rights. It was about Phillips's failure to comply with dominant views. The rush to offense, and from there to legal mechanisms, erodes the informal space in which politics is practiced.

In a diverse society characterized by difference and disagreement, politics depends on a civic spirit according to which we are not eager either to be offended or to press our grievances in lawsuits. It is difficult to institutionalize that solution. One can imagine a legal doctrine according to which the courts refuse to take cases that could be settled informally, but it is immensely difficult to craft one. Courts already toss out frivolous suits or refer others for mediation. One struggles to conjure an applicable standard beyond prudential judgment for when the court should not take cases. (In *Masterpiece Cakeshop,* the Court was hearing an appeal from a state body that had already taken up the case.) In the end, a civic culture that ennobles politics is the only solution. It is possible that a large and diverse society cannot share a civic culture, which is less a case against civic culture than against the feasibility of a large and diverse society, for a society that cannot share basic public commitments amid pluralism cannot cohere as a society. That would be a decidedly un-Madisonian position. He felt a large republic was not only possible but also the key to inhibiting majoritarian abuses.

It is that ethic of politics well understood—not power games, but a shared pursuit of meaningful goods—that republican constitutionalism seeks to restore. It demands not so much self-restraint from judges as a fully operating mechanism of separation of powers to which they are subject. Such a mechanism can inhibit bad judicial behavior as much as correcting or punishing it. The real problem is not its infrequent use but its complete absence. Judicial finality makes judges independent of the people and thus induces them to think they are absolute or infallible.

But it is not just their arrogance we should fear. It is our own isolation. A system of judicial supervision of the rights of individuals is precisely the kind of regime Thomas Hobbes envisioned and that Aristotle and Tocqueville feared: one in which people are isolated from each other and dependent on the ruling element for protection. Hobbes is remembered as an apologist for absolutism, but he is more important as the first philosopher of isolation. Aristotle and Tocqueville showed that a flattened system of disconnected individuals superintended by a government that they regard as foreign to them is conducive to tyranny. It is also hostile to our political natures and thus to many of our highest goods.

Before blaming elites, we should pause to note that the people's indifference to constitutionalism, which their elected representatives reflect, has opened the field to judges. Madison's theory of establishing constitutional meaning by settled practice thus poses a serious problem:

there is also, as Richard Epstein notes, a sustained consensus in favor of deference to courts. But a people who has reached this consensus can undo it too; Madison only requires that change achieved by this method command widespread assent arising from its slow and deliberate nature. Reversing judicial supremacy will be like turning a battleship: slow and difficult, but obviously attainable. And it must be. Only a people that cares not just what happens but how it happens can maintain constitutional government.

We cannot look to the courts for an abstract conception of justice, as Eugene Hickok and Gary L. McDowell note, only for the interpretation of law: "What was once a debate about how to interpret the law and the Constitution has become a debate over whether or not judges should let the law or the Constitution get in the way of doing the right thing. A concern that judges interpret law and be bound by it has run up against the demand that justice be done and that judges do it."[59] To say otherwise is to invest judges with unchecked power, which would in turn encourage them to behave, as Brutus warned, as though they were "independent of heaven itself." Republican constitutionalism neither deprecates the proper role of courts in applying the law to individual cases, nor denies that the Constitution places some issues beyond the community's transient reach. But the space it leaves for the operation of politics of obligation, nobly conceived and mediated by the res publica, is more capacious. It should be renewed.

Notes

INTRODUCTION

1. James Bradley Thayer, "The Origin and Scope of the American Doctrine of Constitutional Law," *Harvard Law Review* 7, no. 3 (1893): 129–156; Robert H. Bork, *The Tempting of America: The Political Seduction of the Law* (New York: Simon & Schuster, 2009); Raoul Berger, *Government by Judiciary: The Transformation of the Fourteenth Amendment*, 2nd ed. (Indianapolis: Liberty Fund, 1997); Larry D. Kramer, *The People Themselves: Popular Constitutionalism and Judicial Review* (New York: Oxford University Press, 2004); Lino Graglia, "Constitutional Law without the Constitution: The Supreme Court's Remaking of America," in Robert H. Bork, ed., *A Country I Do Not Recognize* (Stanford, CA: Hoover Institution Press, 2005); Christopher Wolfe, *The Rise of Modern Judicial Review: From Judicial Interpretation to Judge-Made Law* (New York: Rowman & Littlefield, 1994); George Thomas, *The Madisonian Constitution* (Baltimore: Johns Hopkins University Press, 2008); Benjamin A. Kleinerman, "The Madisonian Constitution: Rightly Understood," *Texas Law Review* 90, no. 4 (2012): 943–972; Eugene W. Hickok and Gary McDowell, *Justice vs. Law: Courts and Politics in American Society* (New York: Free Press, 1993); Robert P. George, *The Clash of Orthodoxies: Law, Religion, and Morality in Crisis* (Wilmington, DE: ISI Books, 2001); John Agresto, *The Supreme Court and Constitutional Democracy* (Ithaca, NY: Cornell University Press, 1984); J. Harvie Wilkinson III, *Cosmic Constitutional Theory: Why Americans Are Losing Their Inalienable Right to Self-Government* (New York: Oxford University Press, 2012); James R. Stoner, "Who Has Authority over the Constitution of the United States?" in Steven Kautz, Arthur Melzer, et al., eds., *The Supreme Court and the Idea of Constitutionalism* (Philadelphia: University of Pennsylvania Press, 2009); Matthew J. Franck, *Against the Imperial Judiciary: The Supreme Court vs. the Sovereignty of the People* (Lawrence: University Press of Kansas, 1996); and Mark Pulliam, "Unleashing the 'Least Dangerous' Branch: Quis Custodiet Ipsos Custodes?" *Texas Review of Law and Politics* 22, no. 3 (Spring 2018): 423–468.

2. I deal with Barnett and Sandefur at length in chapter 4. For the others, see Steven G. Calabresi, "Thayer's Clear Mistake," *Northwestern University Law Review* 88 (1993): 269–277; Richard A. Posner, "The Rise and Fall of Judicial Self-Restraint," *California Law Review* 100 (2012): 519–556; Tara Smith, "Reckless Caution: The Perils of Judicial Minimalism," *NYU Journal of Law & Liberty*

5 (2010): 347–393; Richard A. Epstein, *The Classical Liberal Constitution: The Uncertain Quest for Limited Government* (Cambridge: Harvard University Press, 2014) and *Supreme Neglect: How to Revive Constitutional Protection for Private Property* (New York: Oxford University Press, 2008); and John O. McGinnis, "The Duty of Clarity," *George Washington Law Review* 84, no. 4 (2016): 834–919.

3. George Thomas, "Recovering the Political Constitution: The Madisonian Vision," *The Review of Politics* 66, no. 2 (Spring 2004): 233–256.

4. Keith Whittington, *Constitutional Construction: Divided Powers and Constitutional Meaning* (Cambridge: Harvard University Press, 2001), 1.

5. Corina Barrett Lain, "Upside-Down Judicial Review," *Georgetown Law Journal* 101 (2012): 113–184, https://georgetownlawjournal.org/articles/147/upside-down-judicial-review.

6. Kautz, *Supreme Court and the Idea of Constitutionalism*, 97.

CHAPTER 1. A REPUBLICAN CONSTITUTION

1. Robert H. Bork, "Natural Law and the Constitution," *First Things* (March 1992), https://www.firstthings.com/article/1992/03/natural-law-and-the-constitution.

2. Barack Obama, "State of the Union Address" (speech, Jan 27, 2010), https://obamawhitehouse.archives.gov/photos-and-video/video/2010-state-union-address#transcript.

3. Citizens United v. Federal Election Commission, 558 U.S. 310 (2010).

4. Adam Liptak, "Supreme Court Gets a Rare Rebuke, in Front of a Nation," *New York Times,* January 28, 2010, A12.

5. James McClellan and George W. Carey, eds., *The Federalist: The Gideon Edition* (Indianapolis: Liberty Fund, 2001), 268. References to *The Federalist* are hereafter cited by essay and page number, as in "*Federalist* 51:268."

6. *Federalist* 78:402.

7. *Federalist* 78:404.

8. Christopher Wolfe, ed., *That Eminent Tribunal: Judicial Supremacy and the Constitution* (Princeton, NJ: Princeton University Press, 2004), 152.

9. Benjamin Kleinerman, "The Madisonian Constitution," *Texas Law Review* 943 (2011–2012): 961.

10. Larry D. Kramer, *The People Themselves: Popular Constitutionalism and Judicial Review* (New York: Oxford University Press), 8. I do not mean by this distinction to suggest a fundamental disagreement with Kramer, only a different inflection. But the inflection is important. Kramer's opening illustrations of early American practice, for example, all feature citizens animated by populism and

acting directly through jury decisions, demonstrations, and the like. While I do not deny the importance of such forums and their value, particularly juries, the normal case should be contestation of constitutional meaning that is "refine[d] and enlarge[d]," as Federalist no. 10 says, through elected representatives.

11. Kramer, 24.

12. James W. Ceaser, "Restoring the Constitution," *Claremont Review of Books* 12, no. 2 (Spring 2012).

13. Randy E. Barnett, *Our Republican Constitution: Securing the Liberty and Sovereignty of We the People* (New York: Broadside Books, 2016), 22. Barnett's "bind in conscience" formulation follows Aquinas, as he indicates in *Restoring the Lost Constitution* (Princeton: Princeton University Press: 2003) 50, n. 48.

14. John Locke, *Second Treatise*, par. 131. See David Wooton, ed., *John Locke: Political Writings* (Indianapolis: Hackett Publishing, 2003), 327.

15. *Federalist* 78:404.

16. *Federalist* 53:277.

17. Barnett, *Our Republican Constitution,* 18–28.

18. James Madison, Madison to Vermont Governor Jonas Galusha, November 30, 1812, in *The Papers of James Madison,* Presidential Series, J. C. A. Stagg et al., eds. (Charlottesville, VA: University of Virginia Press, 2004) 5: 472.

19. James Madison, "Majority Governments," in *The Writings of James Madison*, Gaillard Hunt, ed. (New York: G.P. Putnam, 1910), 9: 520.

20. Adam J. White, "Against Judicial Exceptionalism," paper presented at the 2017 American Political Science Association Meeting, San Francisco; Barnett, *Restoring the Lost Constitution.* It should be noted, as I shall explore in more detail below, that Barnett casts his presumption of liberty as a rule for construing the Constitution where its meaning cannot be definitively ascertained through interpretation, not as a rule for interpretation more broadly.

21. Clark M. Neily III, *Terms of Engagement: How Our Courts Should Enforce the Constitution's Promise of Limited Government* (New York: Encounter Books, 2013), 2.

22. Neily, 13.

23. Daniel McInerny, ed., *The Common Things: Essays on Thomism and Education* (Mishawaka, IN.: American Maritain Association, 1999), see chap. 4.

24. Robert Nisbet, *The Quest for Community* (Wilmington, DE: Intercollegiate Studies Institute, 2010).

25. Robert Dahl, *A Preface to Democratic Theory* (Chicago: The University of Chicago Press, 1956), 6.

26. Plato, *The Last Days of Socrates* (New York: Penguin Books, 2010), 51e.

27. Daniel J. Mahoney, "Beyond the 'Prison of the Corollaries': Liberty and the Common Good in the Thought of Bertrand de Jouvenel," *First Prin-*

ciples (January 1, 2008), http://www.firstprinciplesjournal.com/print.aspx?arti
cle=1586&loc=b&type=cbbp, accessed May 6, 2018.

28. Edmund Burke, "Appeal from the New to the Old Whigs," in Daniel E. Ritchie, ed., *Further Reflections on the Revolution in France* (Indianapolis: Liberty Fund, 1992), 161.

29. Barnett, *Restoring the Lost Constitution*, 13.

30. Barnett, *Our Republican Constitution*, 19.

31. Barnett, *Restoring the Lost Constitution*, see 9–12.

32. For Mark Tushnet, see *Taking the Constitution Away from the Courts* (NJ: Princeton University Press, 2000). For Bork, see, for example, Barnett's reference to him as a "moral nihilist," in Randy Barnett, "Ed Whelan vs George Will on 'Judicial Restraint,'" *The Volokh Conspiracy*, October 23, 2015, https://www.washingtonpost.com/news/volokh-conspiracy/wp/2015/10/23/ed-whelan-vs-george-will-on-judicial-restraint/?utm_term=.1a701b698a39, accessed August 28, 2017.

33. Bork's fullest statement of his judicial philosophy is his *The Tempting of America: The Political Seduction of the Law* (New York: Free Press, 1997), in which he specifically contrasts positivism with moral relativism. For "all law," see p. 122. Further, see his discussion of *Bakke* as well as the privatization of morality on pp. 245 and 246, ff.

34. Robert Bork, "Neutral Principles and Some First Amendment Problems," *Indiana Law Journal* 47, no. 1 (1971), 10.

35. J. Harvie Wilkinson, *Cosmic Constitutional Theory: Why Americans Are Losing Their Inalienable Right to Self-Governance* (New York: Oxford University Press, 2012).

36. Tara Smith, "Reckless Caution," *NYU Journal of Law and Liberty* 5, 363–365. Smith's argument is directed to "minimalism," the idea that judges should proceed by degrees rather than in fell swoops. That is different from restraint, but the ideas are related and, absent political grounding, exposed to some of the same difficulties.

37. John Agresto, *The Supreme Court and Constitutional Democracy* (NY: Cornell University Press, 1984), 146.

38. Kramer, *The People Themselves*, 24.

39. Stephen Breyer, *Active Liberty: Interpreting Our Democratic Constitution* (New York: Vintage Books, 2005), 48–49.

40. John Hart Ely, *Democracy and Distrust: A Theory of Judicial Review* (Cambridge, MA: Harvard University Press, 1980). See also Wilkinson's perceptive critique of Ely in *Cosmic Constitutional Theory*, chap. 3.

41. Thomas Jefferson to Henry Lee, May 8, 1825, in Paul Leicester Ford, ed.,

The Works of Thomas Jefferson in Twelve Volumes (New York: G. P. Putnam, 1905), 12: 409.

42. *The Madisonian Constitution, 6–7.*

43. Cooper v. Aaron, 358 U.S. 18 (1958).

44. See Louis Fisher, *Congress: Protecting Individual Rights* (Lawrence : University Press of Kansas, 2016). Kramer has argued persuasively that the stakes of this debate about judicial assertiveness or restraint are heightened by the false need for ultimate judicial settlement of constitutional questions. There is, after all, more space for judges to engage if their word is not final and incontestable. See Larry D. Kramer, "Popular Constitutionalism, circa 2004," *California Law Review* 92 no. 4 (July 2004), 987–990.

45. Christopher Wolfe, *The Rise of Modern Judicial Review: From Judicial Interpretation to Judge-Made Law* (New York: Rowman and Littlefield, 1994), 36.

46. Timothy Sandefur, *The Conscience of the Constitution: The Declaration of Independence and the Right to Liberty* (Washington: Cato Institute, 2014), 158.

47. Sandefur, *The Conscience of the Constitution*, 111.

48. Alexis de Tocqueville, *Democracy in America* (Chicago: University of Chicago Press, 2002), 663.

49. Learned Hand, *The Bill of Rights* (Cambridge, MA: Harvard University Press, 1958), 73.

50. Keith E. Whittington, *Constitutional Construction: Divided Powers and Constitutional Meaning* (Cambridge, MA: Harvard University Press, 2001).

51. This is true even with respect to the exercise of rights. See, inter alia, Akhil Reed Amar, *The Bill of Rights: Creation and Reconstruction* (New Haven, CT: Yale University Press, 1998).

52. Steven Kautz et al., *The Supreme Court and the Idea of Constitutionalism* (Philadelphia: University of Pennsylvania Press, 1980), 235.

53. On the Ninth Amendment as a rule of construction rather than a limitless source of undefined individual rights, see Kurt Lash, *The Lost History of the Ninth Amendment* (New York: Oxford University Press, 2009).

54. *Federalist* 49:262.

55. Barnett thus writes: "[T]here are not one but two sources of binding laws: laws that are produced by unanimous consent regimes, and laws that are produced by regimes whose legitimacy rests solely on their procedural assurances that the rights of the nonconsenting persons on whom they are imposed have been protected." Barnett, *Restoring the Lost Constitution*, 46.

56. Cohens v. Virginia, 19 U.S. 264 (1821) at 405. See also Matthew J. Franck, *Against the Imperial Judiciary: The Supreme Court vs. the Sovereignty of the People* (Lawrence: University Press of Kansas, 1996), 72.

57. Roger Pilon, "Rethinking Judicial Restraint," *Wall Street Journal*, February 1, 1991, available at https://www.cato.org/publications/commentary/re thinking-judicial-restraint. For a fuller explication, see Roger Pilon, "Freedom, Responsibility, and the Constitution: On Recovering Our Founding Principles," *Notre Dame Law Review* 68 (1993): 507.

CHAPTER 2. THE POLITICS OF OBLIGATION

1. Edmund Burke, *Reflections on the Revolution in France* (Indianapolis: Liberty Fund, 1999), 191.

2. Thomas Jefferson to James Madison, September 6, 1789, 382–387, in Charles F. Hobson Robert A. Rutland, et. al., eds., *The Papers of James Madison* (Charlottesville, VA: University of Virginia Press, 1979), 12: 382–387 (emphasis in original. Ilan Wurman uses the exchange as the basis of his compelling book *A Debt Against the Living: An Introduction to Originalism* (New York: Cambridge University Press, 2017) but still casts the question of authority in presentist terms: "Is the Constitution a good constitution worthy of our continued obedience today?" (See p. 5.)

3. James Madison to Thomas Jefferson, February 4, 1790, in Robert A. Rutland et. al., eds., *The Papers of James Madison* (Charlottesville, VA: University of Virginia Press, 1981), 13: 19.

4. Jesse Merriam, "Originalism's Legal Turn as a Libertarian Turn," *Online Library of Law and Liberty,* May 8, 2018, accessed May 8, 2018, http://www.liber tylawsite.org/2018/05/08/libertarian-originalism/.

5. Eugene W. Hickok and Gary L. McDowell, *Justice vs. Law* (New York: Free Press 1993), 196.

6. Clark M. Neily III, *Terms of Engagement: How Our Courts Should Enforce the Constitution's Promise of Limited Government* (New York: Encounter Books, 2013), 2.

7. Timothy Sandefur, *The Conscience of the Constitution: The Declaration of Independence and the Right to Liberty* (Washington: Cato Institute, 2014), 141–142.

8. Aristotle, *Aristotle's Politics: Second Edition*, Carnes Lord, ed. (Chicago: University of Chicago Press, 2013), 3: 11 (1281b).

9. See Willmoore Kendall, *John Locke and the Doctrine of Majority-Rule* (Champaign: University of Illinois Press, 1959).

10. Randy E. Barnett and Evan Bernick, "The Letter and the Spirit: The Judicial Duty of Good-Faith Constitutional Construction," *Georgetown Law* (2017), https://scholarship.law.georgetown.edu/facpub/1946/, 19.

11. John Locke, *Second Treatise,* David Wooton, ed., *John Locke: Political Writings* (Indianapolis: Hackett Publishing, 2003),, 305 (para. 89).

12. Thomas Hobbes, *Leviathan* (New York: Cambridge University Press, 1996). See also Jean-Jaques Rousseau, "Discourse on Inequality" and "The Social Contract," both in John T. Scott, ed., *The Major Political Writings of Jean-Jacques Rousseau* (Chicago: University of Chicago Press, 2012).

13. Burke, *Reflections,* 364.

14. Burke, *Reflections,* 151 (emphasis in original).

15. Burke, *Reflections,* 155.

16. Peter J. Stanlis, *Edmund Burke and the Natural Law* (New Brunswick, NJ: Transaction Publishers, 2003).

17. Burke, *Reflections,* 192–93.

18. Burke, *Reflections,* 191.

19. Burke, *Reflections,* 121–122. Cf. Thomas Aquinas: "[T]hose who first set out to discover something useful for the community of mankind, because they were not themselves able to take everything into account, made certain imperfect arrangements which were deficient in many ways; and these were changed by their successors, who made other arrangements which would fail to secure the common welfare in fewer cases." In R. W. Dyson, ed., *Aquinas: Political Writings* (New York: Cambridge University Press, 2002), 150.

20. Randy E. Barnett, *Our Republican Constitution: Securing the Liberty and Sovereignty of We the People* (New York: Broadside Books, 2016), 22. Barnett's "bind in conscience" formulation follows Aquinas, as he indicates in *Restoring the Lost Constitution* (Princeton: Princeton University Press: 2003), 28 (emphasis added).

21. Hadley Arkes, *Beyond the Constitution* (Princeton: Princeton University Press, 1990), 14.

22. Edwin Meese, "The Law of the Constitution," *Tulane Law Review* 61 (1986–1987): 984.

23. *Aquinas: Political Writings,* 41.

24. See J. Budziszewski, *Commentary on Thomas Aquinas' Virtue Ethics* (New York: Cambridge University Press, 2017), 88.

25. *Federalist* 49:262.

26. Sandefur, *Conscience of the Constitution,* 7.

27. Sandefur, *Conscience of the Constitution,* 2.

28. To be sure, that to which we defer may itself be theoretically grounded. I believe the American Founding is more variegated than that, but the point here is the relentlessness of the demand that the regime correspond with philosophical standards. We can still respect out of habit a regime that began in philosophy.

29. John O. McGinnis and Michael B. Rappaport, *Originalism and the Good Constitution* (Cambridge, MA: Harvard University Press, 2013), 1 ("Law in general . . . ") and 19 ("Our normative approach . . . ").

30. Keith E. Whittington, *Constitutional Interpretation: Textual Meaning, Original Intent, and Judicial Review* (Lawrence: University Press of Kansas, 1999), 135.

31. Learned Hand, *The Bill of Rights* (Cambridge, MA: Harvard University Press, 1958), 15.

32. Hand, *Bill of Rights*, 29–30.

33. William H. Pryor Jr., "The Unbearable Rightness of *Marbury v. Madison*: Its Real Lessons and Irrepressible Myths," *Engage* 12, no. 2 (September 2011).

34. Hand, *Bill of Rights*, 39.

35. Hand, *Bill of Rights*, 46.

36. Hand, *Bill of Rights*, 50–51.

37. Hand, *Bill of Rights*, 70. Hand also predicted, prophetically, that making judges a third chamber would bitterly politicize their nominations before the Senate.

38. Felix Frankfurter and Adrian S. Fisher, "The Business of the Supreme Court at the October Terms, 1935 and 1936," *Harvard Law Review* 51, no. 4 (February 1938), 623.

39. Frankfurter, "The Business of the Supreme Court," 626. For *Fletcher v. Peck:* 10 U.S. 87 (1810).

40. Felix Frankfurter, "John Marshall and the Judicial Function," *Harvard Law Review* 69, no. 2 (December 1955): 217-238.

41. Frankfurter, "John Marshall and the Judicial Function," 225.

42. Frankfurter, "John Marshall and the Judicial Function," 228.

43. Frankfurter, "John Marshall and the Judicial Function," 230.

44. Frankfurter, "John Marshall and the Judicial Function," 235.

45. Frankfurter, "John Marshall and the Judicial Function," 237.

46. Frankfurter, "John Marshall and the Judicial Function," 238.

47. West Virginia State Board of Education v. Barnette, 319 U.S. 624 (1943).

48. Mapp v. Ohio, 367 U.S. 643 (1961).

49. Alexander M. Bickel, *The Least Dangerous Branch: The Supreme Court at the Bar of Politics* (New Haven, CT: Yale University Press, 1986), 1.

50. Bickel, *The Least Dangerous Branch*, 15.

51. Bickel, *The Least Dangerous Branch*, 16 ("counter-majoritarian"), 18 ("deviant institution"), chap. 4 ("passive virtues").

52. Bickel, *The Least Dangerous Branch*, 125–126.

53. Bickel, *The Least Dangerous Branch*, 133.

54. Poe v. Ullman, 367 U.S. 497 (1961).

55. Bickel, *The Least Dangerous Branch*, 155.

56. Bickel, *The Least Dangerous Branch*, 156.

57. Garner v. Louisiana, 368 U.S. 157 (1961).

58. *Federalist* 49:262 (emphasis in original).

59. See George W. Carey and Greg Weiner, "The Founding Fathers: A Conserving Caucus in Action," *Modern Age* 56, no. 1 (Winter 2014), 29–41.

60. Burke, *Reflections*, 363–364.

61. Burke, *Reflections*, 191.

CHAPTER 3. MADISON'S JUDGES

1. Gaillard Hunt, ed., *The Writings of James Madison* (New York: G. P. Putnam, 1910), 9: 66.

2. Spencer Roane, "On the Lottery Decision" (1861) in Howard Gillman, Mark A. Graber, and Keith E. Whittington, eds., *American Constitutionalism: Powers, Rights, and Liberties* (New York: Oxford University Press, 2014), chap. 4, available at http://global.oup.com/us/companion.websites/fdscontent/uscompanion/us/static/companion.websites/gillman/instructor/Chapter_4/roane_sidney_essays_on_the_lottery_decision.pdf.

3. Greg Weiner, *Madison's Metronome: The Constitution, Majority Rule, and the Tempo of American Politics* (Lawrence: University Press of Kansas, 2012) as well as Greg Weiner, "James Madison and the Legitimacy of Majority Factions," *American Political Thought* 2, no. 2 (Fall 2013): 198–216.

4. James Madison to Thomas Jefferson, June 27, 1823, in *The Writings of James Madison*, 9: 143.

5. James Madison to James Monroe, October 5, 1786, in Robert A. Rutland and William M. E. Rachal, eds., *The Papers of James Madison* (Chicago: University of Chicago Press, 1975), 9: 140–142.

6. On these mechanisms, see Weiner, *Madison's Metronome.*

7. Robert A. Rutland and William M. E. Rachal, eds., *The Papers of James Madison* (Chicago: University of Chicago Press, 1973), 8: 298–304.

8. Greg Weiner, "After Federalist No. 10," *National Affairs* (Fall 2017).

9. Hunt, *The Writings of James Madison*, 9: 58.

10. The letter does not appear in the Gaillard Hunt *The Writings of James Madison* collection. See Drew McCoy, *The Last of the Fathers: James Madison and the Republican Legacy* (New York: Cambridge University Press, 1991), 117.

11. Hunt, *Writings of James Madison*, 9: 287.

12. James Burns, *Deadlock of Democracy: Four-Party Politics in America* (New York: Prentice-Hall, 1963).

13. George W. Carey, "Separation of Powers and the Madisonian Model: A Reply to the Critics," *American Political Science Review* 72, no. 1 (August 1978): 151–164.

14. See George W. Carey, "Majority Rule and the Extended Republic Theory of James Madison," in George W. Carey, *In Defense of the Constitution* (Indianapolis: Liberty Fund, 1997), 34–52.

15. Michael Zuckert argues that the Constitutional Convention's rejection of a series of political institutions Madison proposed—the Council of Revision and the Congressional veto over state laws for purposes of both federalism and individual rights within the states—eventuated in the transfer of such mechanisms of constitutional review to the judiciary. Michael Zuckert, "Natural Rights and Modern Constitutionalism," *Northwestern Journal of International Human Rights* 2, no. 1 (Spring 2004).

16. Robert Bork, *The Tempting of America: The Political Seduction of the Law* (New York: Free Press, 1990), 139.

17. Alexander M. Bickel, *The Least Dangerous Branch: The Supreme Court at the Bar of Politics* (New Haven, CT: Yale University Press, 1986).

18. Robert A. Rutland, Charles F. Hobson, et. al., eds., *The Papers of James Madison* (Charlottesville: University of Virginia Press, 1977), 11:293.

19. Charles S. Hobson, Robert A. Rutland, et. al., *The Papers of James Madison* (Charlottesville: University of Virginia Press, 1979), 12:232–233.

20. *Federalist* 84: 447.

21. David B. Mattern, J. C. A. Stagg, et. al., eds., *The Papers of James Madison*, (Charlottesville: University of Virginia Press, 1991), 17:312.

22. William T. Hutchinson and William M. E. Rachal, eds., *The Papers of James Madison* (Chicago: University of Chicago Press, 1962), 2:366.

23. Hunt, *Writings of James Madison*, 9: 397 (emphasis added).

24. *Federalist* 37:183.

25. Gaillard Hunt, ed., *The Writings of James Madison* (New York: G. P. Putnam, 1906), 8:330. Madison's claim that the ongoing bank controversy was "settled" was, of course questionable as an empirical matter.

26. Richard Epstein, *The Classical Liberal Constitution: The Uncertain Quest for Limited Government* (Cambridge, MA: Harvard University Press, 2017), 86–116.

27. Hunt, *Writings of James Madison*, 9:286–287.

28. Hunt, *Writings of James Madison*, 8:403–407. Emphasis in original. See Zuckert in note 15 above.

29. In 1824, Madison, echoing *Federalist* no. 37, would say that the meaning of the text could not be ascertained by words alone, as opposed to by what those words were understood to mean at the time, because the meanings of words change.

30. Hunt, *Writings of James Madison*, 8:368–388.

31. *Federalist* 39:198.

32. George W. Carey, "Conservatism, Centralization, and Constitutional Federalism," *Modern Age* (Winter/Spring 2004): 48–59.

33. Hunt, *Writings of James Madison,* 9:342–343. Cf. Madison to Jefferson, June 27, 1823, which also refers to *Federalist* 39 as decisive.

34. Hunt, *Writings of James Madison,* 9:116.

35. Hunt, *Writing of James Madison,* 9:141.

36. James Bradley Thayer, "The Origin and Scope of the American Doctrine of Constitutional Law," *Harvard Law Review* 7, no. 3 (October 25, 1893): 129–156.

37. *Federalist* 78:402 (emphasis added).

38. George W. Carey, *In Defense of the Constitution,* Online Library of Liberty (Indianapolis: Liberty Fund, 1989), http://oll.libertyfund.org/titles/678# Carey_0008_444.

39. Matthew J. Franck, *Against the Imperial Judiciary: The Supreme Court vs. the Sovereignty of the People* (Lawrence: University Press of Kansas, 1996), 42.

40. *Federalist* 78:407.

41. *Federalist* 78:407.

42. See Robert H. Bork, ed., *A Country I Do Not Recognize* (Stanford, CA.: Hoover Institution Press, 2005), 7.

43. See also Franck, *Against the Imperial Judiciary,* 40: The reference to "'all acts contrary to the manifest tenor of the Constitution' must be understood by reference to the antecedent examples of 'specified exemptions to the legislative authority.'" In other words, these are cases of a judiciary nature.

44. *Federalist* 78:405.

45. Harlan Fiske Stone, "The Common Law in the United States," *Harvard Law Review* 50, no. 1 (November 1936): 25.

46. *Federalist* 78:406.

47. Alexander Hamilton, "Remarks on an Act for Regulating Elections," *The Founders' Constitution* 5, Amendment V, Document 13 (1787), http://press-pubs .uchicago.edu/founders/documents/amendV_due_processs13.html.

48. *Federalist* 79:409–410.

49. *Federalist* 80:420.

50. *Federalist* 80:416.

51. Akhil Reed Amar, *America's Constitution: A Biography* (New York: Random House, 2005), 215.

52. See, for example, Randy Barnett, *Restoring the Lost Constitution: The Presumption of Liberty* (Princeton: Princeton University Press: 2003), 140.

53. David M. Burke, "The 'Presumption of Constitutionality' Doctrine and the Rehnquist Court: A Lethal Combination for Individual Liberty," *Harvard Journal of Law & Public Policy* 18, no. 1 (Fall 1994).

54. David. J. Siemers, *The Myth of Coequal Branches: Restoring the Constitution's Separation of Functions* (Columbia: University of Missouri Press, 2018), chap. 5.

55. Morton J. Frisch, ed., *The Pacificus-Helvidius Debates of 1793–1794: Toward the Completion of the American Founding* (Indianapolis: Liberty Fund, 2007), 59.

56. See, among others, George W. Carey, *A Student's Guide to American Political Thought* (Wilmington, DE: ISI Books, 2014), ebook.

57. The clearest example is *Federalist* no. 41.

58. Montesquieu, *The Spirit of the Laws* (New York: Cambridge University Press, 2002), 157. On Montesquieu's paramount influence, see Donald Lutz, "The Relative Influence of European Writers on Late Eighteenth-Century American Thought," *American Political Science Review* 78, no. 1 (March 1984): 189–197.

59. Montesquieu, *Spirit of the Laws*, 160.

60. Bruce Frohnen, ed., *The American Republic: Primary Sources* (Indianapolis: Liberty Fund, 2002), 197.

61. Gordon Lloyd, ed., *Debates in the Federal Convention of 1787 by James Madison, a Member* (Ashland, Ohio: Ashbrook Center, 2014). See remarks on June 6.

62. *Federalist* 78:403 (emphasis added). Cf. Larry D. Kramer, *The People Themselves: Popular Constitutionalism and Judicial Review* (New York: Oxford University Press), 250: "How ironic if the only way we can sustain this supposedly weakest branch is by making it the strongest one: letting it order the others about with impunity while forbidding them to resist and insisting that their only recourse is to wait for the Court's members to die or tire of the job."

63. *Federalist* 47:258.

64. *Federalist* 49:261.

65. James Wilson, *Lectures on Law* (Clark, NJ: The Lawbook Exchange, 2005), 1: 455.

66. St. George Tucker, *View of the Constitution of the United States and Selected Writings* (Indianapolis: Liberty Fund, 1999), http://oll.libertyfund.org/titles/693#Tucker_0023_682.

67. James Kent, *Commentaries on American Law* (Boston: Little, Brown, and Company, 1896), Kindle edition, location 40719.

68. Kent, *Commentaries on American Law*, location 34119.

69. Kramer, *The People Themselves*, 145.

70. Kramer, 146.

71. *Federalist* 78:404.

72. *Trademark Cases*, 100 U.S. 95–96 (1879).

73. Thayer, "The Origin and Scope of the American Doctrine of Constitutional Law."

74. John O. McGinnis, "The Duty of Clarity," *George Washington Law Review* 84, no. 4 (August 2016): 843.

75. Richard Posner, "The Rise and Fall of Judicial Self-Restraint," *California Law Review* 100, no. 3 (2012): 538–540.

76. Joseph Story, *Commentaries on the Constitution of the United States* (New Orleans, Quid Pro Quo Books, 2013), §163. See also Franck, *Against the Imperial Judiciary*, 88–89.

77. Story, *Commentaries*, §374.

78. Story, *Commentaries*, §375.

79. Michael Stokes Paulsen, "The *Merryman* Power and the Dilemma of Autonomous Executive Branch Interpretation," *Cardozo Law Review* 15, no. 81 (1993–1994).

80. Marbury v. Madison, 5 U.S. 177 (1803).

81. Don E. Fehrenbacher, ed., *Abraham Lincoln: Speeches & Writings 1859–1865* (New York: Library of America, 1989), iBooks edition. See also Michael Stokes Paulsen, "Lincoln and Judicial Authority," *Notre Dame Law Review* 83 (2008): 1227.

CHAPTER 4. THE ANTIPOLITICAL CONSTITUTION

1. Randy Barnett, *Restoring the Lost Constitution: The Presumption of Liberty* (Princeton: Princeton University Press: 2003), 31.

2. Korematsu v. United States, 323 U.S. 214 (1944).

3. McGowan v. Maryland, 366 U.S. 420 (1961).

4. "Massachusetts Blue Laws," Mass.gov, https://www.mass.gov/service-details/massachusetts-blue-laws.

5. McGowan v. Maryland, 445.

6. McGowan v. Maryland, 444.

7. McGowan v. Maryland, 439.

8. McGowan v. Maryland, 466.

9. McGowan v. Maryland, 477.

10. McGowan v. Maryland, 507 ("heritage") and 515 ("atmosphere of general repose").

11. McGowan v. Maryland, 515 ("reintroduce[d]") and 524 ("atmosphere").

12. McGowan v. Maryland, 561.

13. McGowan v. Maryland, 573, n. 6.

14. Mark Pulliam, "Unleashing the 'Least Dangerous' Branch: Quis Custo-

diet Ipsos Custodes?," *Texas Review of Law and Politics* 22, no. 3 (Spring 2018): 443.

15. Randy Barnett, *The Structure of Liberty: Justice and the Rule of Law* (New York: Oxford University Press, 1998), 24 (emphasis added). See also Barnett, *Restoring the Lost Constitution,* 82–83.

16. I shall discuss this claim more extensively in treating the *Slaughter-House Cases* in chap. 5 below. I am unaware of Barnett commenting specifically on *Mc-Gowan,* though he does criticize 1887's *Mugler v. Kansas,* which upheld "safety, health, or morals" legislation under the Fourteenth Amendment. He writes: "By this rationale, courts upheld the power of states to prohibit gambling, the consumption of alcohol, prostitution, doing business on the Sabbath, and other types of activities that did not violate the rights of others" (Barnett, *Restoring the Lost Constitution,* 332). But laws do not exist merely to provide protection amid the war of all individuals against all individuals. They can serve the purpose, as we have seen, of fostering an environment that encourages the community's moral judgments.

17. Thomas Aquinas, *Aquinas: Political Writings,* R. W. Dyson, ed. (New York: Cambridge University Press: 2002), 106.

18. Barnett, *Restoring the Lost Constitution,* 44–45.

19. Barnett, *Restoring the Lost Constitution,* 54.

20. Barnett, *Restoring the Lost Constitution,* 80.

21. For Kurt T. Lash, see *The Lost History of the Ninth Amendment* (New York: Oxford University Press, 2009) and *The Fourteenth Amendment and the Privileges and Immunities of American Citizenship* (New York: Cambridge University Press, 2014). For Barnett's view, see, *inter alia, Our Republican Constitution: Securing the Liberty and Sovereignty of We the People* (New York: Broadside Books, 2016), 106.

22. Raoul Berger, "Ninth Amendment," *Cornell Law Review* 66, no.1 (1980): 1–2 and 8, ff.

23. Larry D. Kramer, *The People Themselves: Popular Constitutionalism and Judicial Review* (New York: Oxford University Press), 44.

24. Wallace Mendelson, "Ninth Amendment Rights and Wrongs—A Note on Noninterpretism," *Political Science Quarterly* 110, no. 3 (Autumn 1995): 411–412.

25. Richard M. Reinsch II, "Dissenting from Natural Rights Nationalism: A Reply to Randy Barnett," *Online Library of Law and Liberty* (February 2015), http://www.libertylawsite.org/2015/02/05/dissenting-from-natural-rights-na tionalism-a-reply-to-randy-barnett/ ("Natural Rights Nationalism"); and Barnett, *Our Republican Constitution* ("Fundamental Rights Federalism"): 197.

26. Mendelson, "Ninth Amendment Rights and Wrongs," 409.

27. Raoul Berger, *Government by Judiciary: The Transformation of the Four-*

teenth Amendment (Cambridge, MA: Harvard University Press, 1977), especially chap. 3.

28. Berger, *Government by Judiciary*, 83.

29. Barnett, *Restoring the Lost Constitution*, 89.

30. Barnett, *Restoring the Lost Constitution*, 114.

31. Alexander M. Bickel, *The Least Dangerous Branch: The Supreme Court at the Bar of Politics* (New Haven, CT: Yale University Press, 1986), 94–95.

32. Barnett, *Restoring the Lost Constitution*, 144–145.

33. Barnett, *Restoring the Lost Constitution*, 82.

34. Barnett, *Restoring the Lost Constitution*, 182.

35. Barnett, *Restoring the Lost Constitution*, 182.

36. Barnett, *Restoring the Lost Constitution*, 192.

37. Michael W. McConnell, "Institutions and Interpretation: A Critique of *City of Boerne v. Flores*," *Harvard Law Review* 111 no. 153 (1997): 166.

38. Barnett quotation from *Restoring the Lost Constitution*, 180; Thomas Jefferson to Spencer Roane, September 6, 1819, *The Founders' Constitution*, http://press-pubs.uchicago.edu/founders/documents/a1_8_18s16.html.

39. James Madison, "Virginia Report of 1800," in Gaillard Hunt, ed., *The Writings of James Madison* (New York: G.P. Putnam, 1906), 307–351.

40. *The Papers of James Madison*, 17: 312.

41. Slaughter-House Cases, 83 U.S. 36 (1873).

42. Barnett, *Restoring the Lost Constitution*, 202 ("require[s]") and 209 ("using the Due Process Clause"). The appellants in *McGowan* likely claimed an Equal Protection violation instead because the Privileges and Immunities clause had long been a constitutional dead letter.

43. Barnett, *Restoring the Lost Constitution*, 209.

44. Barnett, *Restoring the Lost Constitution*, 5.

45. Lochner v. New York is at 198 U.S. 45 (1905). For the definitive revisionist reading, see David Bernstein, *Rehabilitating Lochner: Defending Individual Rights Against Progressive Reform* (Chicago: University of Chicago Press, 2011).

46. Barnett, *Restoring the Lost Constitution*, 216.

47. Barnett, *Restoring the Lost Constitution*, 334.

48. See, *inter alia*, Barnett, *Restoring the Lost Constitution*, 5, and Randy Barnett, "The Proper Scope of the Police Power," *Notre Dame Law Review* 79, no. 429 (February 2004).

49. Barnett, *Restoring the Lost Constitution*, 336.

50. Cf. Chief Justice John Roberts in *Obergefell*: "As Judge Henry Friendly once put it, echoing Justice Holmes' dissent in *Lochner*, the Fourteenth Amendment does not enact John Stuart Mill's *On Liberty* any more than it enacts Herbert Spencer's *Social Statics*."

51. Barnett, *Restoring the Lost Constitution*, 351.

52. See, for example, Barnett's discussion of *Lawrence v. Texas* in Barnett, *Restoring the Lost Constitution*, 337, and Justice Scalia's dissent in *Lawrence* (539 U.S. 558 [2003] at 559).

53. See Frank J. Colucci, *Justice Kennedy's Jurisprudence: The Full and Necessary Meaning of Liberty* (Lawrence: University Press of Kansas, 1999).

54. Richard Epstein, *Supreme Neglect: How to Revive Constitutional Protection for Private Property* (New York: Oxford University Press, 2008), 163.

55. Epstein, *Supreme Neglect*, 167.

56. Epstein, *Supreme Neglect*, 9.

57. Epstein, *Supreme Neglect*, 167.

58. Barnett, *The Structure of Liberty*, 19, emphasis in original; Aquinas, *Aquinas: Political Writings*, 144.

59. Aquinas, *Aquinas: Political Writings*, 79.

60. For example, Aquinas says a tyrannical law "is not strictly speaking a law," but is still expected to be obeyed in order that "the citizens should be good." *Aquinas: Political Writings*, 98.

61. Timothy Sandefur, "In Defense of Substantive Due Process, or the Promise of Lawful Rule," *Harvard Journal of Law & Public Policy*, 35 no. 1 (2012): 292.

62. Sandefur, "In Defense of Substantive Due Process," 295.

63. Sandefur, "In Defense of Substantive Due Process," 317.

64. 3 U.S. 386 (1798). See Sandefur, "In Defense of Substantive Due Process," 320–322.

65. See Ronald Dworkin, *Freedom's Law: The Moral Reading of the American Constitution* (Cambridge, MA: Harvard University Press, 1997), 2.

66. Michael W. McConnell, "The Importance of Humility in Judicial Review: A Comment on Ronald Dworkin's 'Moral Reading of the Constitution,'" *Fordham Law Review* 65 (1997): 1269–1293. See pages 1269 ("It is easy . . . ") and 1292 ("We have heard a lot . . . ").

67. Calder v. Bull, 3 U.S. 386 (1798) at 388.

68. Timothy Sandefur, *The Conscience of the Constitution: The Declaration of Independence and the Right to Liberty* (Washington: Cato Institute, 2014), 89.

69. Sandefur, *Conscience of the Constitution*, 323.

70. Michael Oakeshott, *Lectures in the History of Political Thought* (Charlottesville, VA: Imprint Academic, 2005), 471–496. Oakeshott argues that the telocratic mindset is prone to abuse.

71. Louis Fisher, *Congress: Protecting Individual Rights* (Lawrence: University Press of Kansas, 2016).

72. Learned Hand, *The Spirit of Liberty: Papers and Addresses* (New York: Knopf, 1953), 164.

73. *Federalist* 55:291. Another illustration of the *reductio* is supplied by the portion of Chief Justice Roberts's opinion in *National Federation of Independent Business v. Sebelius* (132 S. Ct. 2566) that declined to use the Commerce Clause to sustain a requirement that individuals purchase health care. Roberts employed an analogy by which, if health care could be mandated because the failure to purchase it affects costs for everyone else, so could purchases of broccoli. I have elsewhere called this "the Broccoli Fallacy." See Greg Weiner, "Roberts' Rules for Self-Government," *Online Library of Law and Liberty,* June 30, 2012, http://www.libertylawsite.org/2012/06/30/the-return-to-self-government/. The fallacy is the belief that the Supreme Court could rescue a nation so sunk into soft despotism that it permits Congress to mandate its diet. These are political, not judicial, arguments. As Roberts also said in the opinion, as will be seen in chap. 5 below, it is not the function of the courts to save us from silliness.

74. Weiner, "Roberts' Rules for Self-Government," 324–325.

75. Lawrence v. Texas, 599.

76. Robert Bork, *The Tempting of America: The Political Seduction of the Law* (New York: Free Press, 1990), 246.

77. Randy Barnett, *Our Republican Constitution,* 124.

78. Barnett, *Our Republican Constitution,* 231.

79. Barnett, *Our Republican Constitution,* 232.

80. Jesse Choper argues reasonably enough that, functionally, "the national legislative process conducted by the political branches is not impeccable democracy in action." This is true enough, including for reasons I shall discuss in chap. 5—namely, the sheer scale of legislative activity—but this is the only constitutional process we have for registering majority will. Jesse Choper, *Judicial Review and the National Political Process: A Functional Reconsideration of the Role of the Supreme Court* (Chicago: University of Chicago Press, 1980), iBooks edition. For the quotation above, see Section VI of chap. 1.

81. Barnett, *Our Republican Constitution,* 233.

82. See Ronald J. Pestritto, ed., *Woodrow Wilson: The Essential Political Writings* (Lanham, MD: Lexington Books, 2005), 159.

83. Barnett quotation in previous paragraph from *Our Republican Constitution,* 242; Kitchen v. Herbert, 961 F. Supp. 2d 1181 (2013) at 1213.

84. Barnett, *Restoring the Lost Constitution,* 268.

85. Barnett, *Our Republican Constitution,* 245.

86. Adam J. White, Twitter, https://twitter.com/adamjwhitedc/status/80864 8591640301568.

87. Steven G. Calabresi, "Thayer's Clear Mistake," *Northwestern University Law Review* 88 (1993): 273–274.

88. George W. Carey, *In Defense of the Constitution* (Indianapolis: Liberty Fund 1995), see http://oll.libertyfund.org/titles/678#Carey_0008_566.

89. Sandefur, *Conscience of the Constitution*, 3.

90. Sandefur, *Conscience of the Constitution*, 4.

91. Palko v. Connecticut, 302 U.S. 319 at 325.

92. Willmoore Kendall and George W. Carey, *Basic Symbols of the American Political Tradition* (Washington, DC: Catholic University of America Press, 1995).

93. Sandefur, *Conscience of the Constitution*, 5.

94. See Diana Schaub, "Bioethics and the Constitution," *The New Atlantis* (Summer 2004): 59.

95. Sandefur, *Conscience of the Constitution*, 9.

96. Sandefur, *Conscience of the Constitution*, 9.

97. Harry V. Jaffa, *Storm Over the Constitution* (New York: Lexington Books, 1999), 142 ("Declartution") and 147 ("paradoxical").

98. See, for example, *Original Intent and the Framers of the Constitution: A Disputed Question* (Washington, DC: Regnery Publishing, 1994), 43: "Given the many anomalies of the Constitution—and none greater of course than slavery—it is good to have Madison's and Jefferson's word that the principles of the Constitution, the principles of republicanism, nowhere defined in the Constitution itself, are those of the Declaration of Independence."

99. See James Madison to Thomas Jefferson, February 8, 1825, in Gaillard Hunt, ed., *The Writings of James Madison* (New York: G. P. Putnam, 1910), 9: 218-221.

100. Madison to Jefferson, 31.

101. Robert Bork, *Slouching Towards Gomorrah: Modern Liberalism and American Decline* (New York: ReganBooks, 1996).

102. Peter Augustine Lawler, *Modern and American Dignity; Who We Are as Persons, and What That Means for Our Future* (Wilmington, DE: ISI Books, 2014), 8 (ebook).

103. *Federalist* 62:362.

104. Hadley Arkes, "A Culture Corrupted," in the symposium "The End of Democracy? The Judicial Usurpation of Politics," *First Things* (November 1996), https://www.firstthings.com/article/1996/11/the-end-of-democracy-the-judicial-usurpation-of-politics.

105. Hadley Arkes, *The Return of George Sutherland: Restoring a Jurisprudence of Natural Rights* (Princeton, NJ: Princeton University Press, 1994).

106. Hadley Arkes, *Beyond the Constitution* (Princeton, NJ: Princeton University Press, 1992).

107. Madison to Jefferson, 3–5.

108. Leon Kass, *Living a Worthy Life: Finding Meaning in Modern Times* (New York: Encounter Books, 2017), 381–382.

109. Arkes, *Beyond the Constitution*, 52.

110. Barnett, *Restoring the Lost Constitution*, 373.

111. Robert George, *The Clash of Orthodoxies: Law, Religion, and Morality in Crisis* (Wilmington, DE: Intercollegiate Studies Institute, 2001), 10.

112. Kramer, *The People Themselves*, 42–43.

113. McGinnis, "The Duty of Clarity."

114. McGinnis, "The Duty of Clarity," 2.

115. John O. McGinnis and Michael B. Rappaport, "Original Methods Originalism: A New Theory of Interpretation and the Case Against Construction," *Northwestern University Law Review* 103, no. 2 (2009): 751–802.

116. Joseph Story, *Commentaries on the Constitution of the United States* (New Orleans: Quid Pro Quo Books, 2013), §190.

CHAPTER 5. CASES AND CONTROVERSIES

1. Snyder v. Phelps, 131 S. Ct. 1207 (2011) at 1222.

2. Snyder v. Phelps, 1213.

3. Snyder v. Phelps, 1216–17.

4. Snyder v. Phelps, 1222.

5. John O. McGinnis, "The Golden Braid of Liberty and Tradition in America," *Online Library of Law and Liberty*, May 25, 2018, http://www.libertylawsite.org/2018/05/25/the-golden-braid-of-liberty-and-tradition-in-america/.

6. Mary Ann Glendon, *Rights Talk: The Impoverishment of Political Discourse* (New York: Free Press, 1993).

7. For a rich and nuanced treatment, see William H. Pryor, "The Unbearable Rightness of *Marbury v. Madison*," *Engage* 12, no. 2 (September 2011).

8. See *ABA Journal*, April 1982, 386. For a history and critique of jurisdiction stripping, see Max Baucus and Kenneth R. Kay, "The Court Stripping Bills: Their Impact on the Constitution, the Courts, and Congress," *Villanova Law Review* 27, no. 5 (1982): 988–1018. It should not escape notice that Baucus was then a United States Senator undermining the authority of his own branch of government in favor of the judiciary.

9. Employment Division of Oregon v. Smith, 494 U.S. 872 (1990). I argue below that the Court wrongly applied the Fourteenth Amendment in *City of Boerne v. Flores*, which overturned this law with respect to state legislation.

10. For an elucidation of this precedent, see William H. Rehnquist, *Grand*

Inquests: The Historic Impeachments of Justice Samuel Chase and President Andrew Johnson (New York: William Morrow & Co., 1992).

11. Matthew J. Franck, *Against the Imperial Judiciary: The Supreme Court vs. the Sovereignty of the People* (Lawrence: University Press of Kansas, 1996), 50.

12. Anna Palmer, Seung Min Kim, et. al., "Obama to shield 5 million from deportation," *Politico,* November 20, 2014, https://www.politico.com/story/2014/11/obama-immigration-plan-unveil-113022.

13. Kelsey Snell and Abby Phillip, "McConnell: We Don't Have Religious Tests in This Country," *Washington Post,* January 29, 2017, https://www.washingtonpost.com/powerpost/mcconnell-we-dont-have-religious-tests-in-this-country/2017/01/29/03215604-e630-11e6-b82f-687d6e6a3e7c_story.html?utm_term=.29aa6be31374.

14. United States v. Carolene Products Co., 304 U.S. 144 (1938).

15. Larry D. Kramer, *The People Themselves: Popular Constitutionalism and Judicial Review* (New York: Oxford University Press, 2004), 219.

16. Franck, *Against the Imperial Judiciary,* 30.

17. "Governor Henry Clay Warmouth," https://www.nga.org/cms/home/governors/past-governors-bios/page_louisiana/col2-content/main-content-list/title_warmoth_henry.html. For a thorough history, see Ronald M Labbe and Jonathan Lurie, *The Slaughterhouse Cases: Regulation, Reconstruction, and the Fourteenth Amendment* (Lawrence: University Press of Kansas, 2005).

18. Kevin Newsom, "Setting Incorporation Straight: A Reinterpretation of the Slaughter-House Cases," *Yale Law Journal* 109, no. 4: 643–744, see especially 680, ff.

19. Slaughter-House Cases, 83 U.S. 75 (1873).

20. District of Columbia v. Heller, 554 U.S. 570 (2008).

21. Slaughter-House Cases, 71.

22. Slaughter-House Cases, 78.

23. Slaughter-House Cases, 87.

24. Slaughter-House Cases, 87–88.

25. Slaughter-House Cases, 115.

26. Slaughter-House Cases, 116.

27. Slaughter-House Cases, 119.

28. Slaughter-House Cases, 66.

29. Tocqueville, 487.

30. Tocqueville, 487.

31. Brown v. Board of Education, 344 U.S. 483 (1954).

32. Missouri v. Jenkins, 515 U.S. 70 (1955) at 120.

33. Gerald Rosenberg, *The Hollow Hope: Can Courts Bring About Social Change?* (Chicago: University of Chicago Press, 2008). See chap. 2.

34. *Williamson v. Lee Optical,* 348 U.S. 483 (1955) at 487–488.

35. Randy Barnett, *Restoring the Lost Constitution: The Presumption of Liberty* (Princeton: Princeton University Press: 2003), 232.

36. James Bradley Thayer, "The Origin and Scope of the American Doctrine of Constitutional Law," *Harvard Law Review* 7, no. 3 (October 25, 1893), 144.

37. See also Robert W. Bennett, "'Mere' Rationality in Constitutional Law: Judicial Review and Democratic Theory," *California Law Review* 67, no. 5 (September 1979): n. 14 at 1051–1052.

38. Gloucester County School Board v. G. G., 136 S. Ct. 2442 (2016).

39. Auer v. Robbins, 519 U.S. 452 (1997).

40. Gavin Grimm, "I'm transgender and can't use the student bathroom. The Supreme Court could change that," *Washington Post,* October 27, 2016, https://www.washingtonpost.com/opinions/im-transgender-and-cant-use-the -student-bathroom-the-supreme-court-could-change-that/2016/10/27 /19d1a3ae-9bc1-11e6-a0ed-ab0774c1eaa5_story.html?utm_term=.32c59c26970b.

41. Chevron USA Inc. v. Natural Resources Defense Council. Inc., 467 U.S. 837 (1984).

42. See Richard M. Reinsch II and Greg Weiner, "A Return to Constitutionalism," *Online Library of Law and Liberty,* February 2, 2017, http://www.liberty lawsite.org/2017/02/02/a-return-to-constitutionalism/.

43. National Federation of Independent Business v. Sebelius, 132 S. Ct. 2566 (2012) at 2597.

44. National Federation of Independent Business v. Sebelius.

45. King v. Burwell, 135 S. Ct. 475 (2014).

46. A.L.A. Schechter Poultry Corp. v. United States, 295 U.S. 495 (1935).

47. Citizens United v. Federal Election Commission, 558 U.S. 310 (2010).

48. James Madison to James Monroe, October 5, 1786, in Robert A. Rutland and William M. E. Rachal, eds., *The Papers of James Madison* (Chicago: University of Chicago Press, 1975), 9, 17:189.

49. New York Times v. Sullivan, 376 U.S. 269 (1964), quoting Roth v. United States.

50. John Hart Ely, *Democracy and Distrust: A Theory of Judicial Review* (Cambridge, MA: Harvard University Press, 1980), 103.

51. J. Harvie Wilkinson, *Cosmic Constitutional Theory: Why Americans Are Losing Their Inalienable Right to Self-Governance* (New York: Oxford University Press, 2012), 78.

52. City of Boerne v. Flores, 521 U.S. 507 (1997).

53. Michael W. McConnell, "Institutions and Interpretation: A Critique of *City of Boerne v. Flores,*" *Harvard Law Review* 111 (1997-1998): 163.

54. City of Boerne v. Flores, 536 (internal citations omitted).

55. For Corwin, see Matthew J. Franck's introduction to *The Doctrine of Judicial Review: Its Legal and Historical Basis and Other Essays* (Piscataway, NJ: Transaction Publishers, 2014), xxviii; Charles S. Hyneman, *The Supreme Court on Trial* (New York: Atherton Press, 1963), 79–80; and Louis Fisher, *On Appreciating Congress: The People's Branch* (Boulder, CO: Paradigm Publishers, 2010), 60–63.

56. Shelby County v. Holder, 57 U.S. 2 (2013).

57. The remark is on page 47 of the transcript of the argument, available at https://www.supremecourt.gov/oral_arguments/argument_transcripts/2012/12-96_7648.pdf.

58. Town of Greece v. Galloway, 572 U.S. 565 (2014) and Masterpiece Cakeshop v. Colorado Civil Rights Commission, 584 U.S. (2018).

59. Eugene W. Hickok and Gary L. McDowell, *Justice vs. Law* (New York: Free Press 1993), 196.

Index